THE JOURNEY

14 DAYS

Waleed Atrushi

Brilliant Books Literary
137 Forest Park Lane Thomasville
North Carolina 27360 USA

PART ONE

On a hot summer afternoon in 1981, I started my journey. A journey where I faced more than two years of suffering, hard work, fear, and intimidation. I can never forget that day. It was a day of decision-making, where I was caught between how to plan my future and where to go from this point on. I stood with more than 5000 teenagers who were called for military service. This was where I was getting drafted despite being in my senior year in high school, and just toward finishing my last year and was planning to go to college and major in Literature Studies. I was so much into reading and writing and even got into writing short stories. My teacher loved everything I wrote, and oftentimes, he would always brag about my level of commitment toward writing. He enjoyed sharing my writing with my classmates and always told them that one day I would be a good writer and would have a bright future. I felt good and worked harder, but all that was about to end. The Iraqi government and its leader, Saddam Hussein, got into a bloody war with Iran, and this was the beginning of the war between Iraq and Iran, which took 8 years. The Saddam Hussein regime did not care about all of these teenagers. All they cared about was shipping all of us to the war zone. They wanted to deploy us all as soon as possible with little or no training. According to some of the soldiers who witnessed the first phase of war they were saying that some of the teenagers who were deployed to the war were trained for less than a month and put in the war zone with absolutely no knowledge of how to survive or fight back. Saddam's regime's idea of the war is to have a half million soldiers on the battlefield at whatever cost. We didn't have much of a choice. We either had to go to war or they would simply shoot us if we refused to go. There was so much fear, intimidation, and if you didn't obey the government and were not willing to die for it, you were considered a traitor, and they will execute you and make a good example out of you. It's not fun living under these circumstances. You constantly have to be looking around you and hope you never ever say the wrong thing or make the wrong move, or it will end. With all that in mind, I stood out watching these teenagers getting on the military convoy after their names were called one by one. I thought about everything. I'm Kurdish, and being Kurdish in Iraq, you are considered less than a citizen, and the government treated Kurdish people like second-class citizens with no rights whatsoever. At school, we were made fun of by other classmates and everywhere else, and yet we were the bravest and the most loyal, and we proved to the Iraqi people that Kurdish people were the first ones to die and fight hard to the end and despite the way we were treated we always worked harder. Being Kurdish was not easy; I remember when they tortured my father and my uncle, and my father was in and out of jail and was accused of helping the Kurdish rebel. He was beaten and tortured many times; in fact, when he was brought home once, he couldn't lay on his back because the government used the iron steam table to torture him just like ironing a shirt he was laid on his face and was tight down while the use the presser from the steam table on his back. Every time I stop by the dry cleaner to pick up my clothes it reminds me of what my father went through and what we have to go through with our daily routine. My uncle, who was well-educated and involved in the Kurdish political movement, was also tortured many times. I remember the last time I saw him, I was a little kid, but I remember very well that he was beaten so badly that the day they brought him home, he died from suffering. They left him in such bad shape. The question that kept crossing my mind after all the tragedy my family faced was, "Why would I even think about fighting for this regime and becoming part of their army"? "We are considered to be second-class citizens. We have no rights and can't even feel good speaking your language." "Why" was what crossed my mind on that hot summer day Why would I serve this country and die for a regime that doesn't care about its people? I kept telling myself that I was not a coward and that I would love to serve my country if my country believed in our rights and freedom. I kept thinking about all of the hard times all the Kurdish people had gone through. All the thoughts that came across my mind were not to go and be part of the army. No way, and with clear conscience, I will not serve this regime. The official was calling names and as I was experiencing how they were getting in the convoy of military trucks and getting shipped to the camp, suddenly, I heard my name loud and clear. And when there was no response from me, they looked around and repeated the name again, and I pretended that I didn't hear anything than they started calling other names. I stood there and knew in my heart that I was doing the right thing, and that I must find a way to get up north where the Kurdish people lived. I rather live free and fight for my people, and if I die doing that at least I know that I fought for what I believe in. So here's my situation. At this point, I need to stay in hiding until I find a way out of the country. It's not easy; in fact, it's a huge risk to go in hiding especially knowing you have no proof. In the event that you get caught, you might as well kill yourself. Deserting the army is not an easy task. You will be tortured and hunged by the neck. With million thought and ideas running through my mind I needed to do some soul-thinking and find a plan to get out of the country as soon as possible. Getting caught is not an option with the punishment being death. As I stood out there thinking about my future and my family. The police and the military police were looking through all of the people ensuring no one gets away. But I walked away to a little park that was close to the military depot. I walked to a tea stand which is something like a coffee stand, where I purchased a cup of hot tea. Despite the unbearable heat, drinking hot tea in Iraq is part of the culture. It doesn't matter how hot it is. I needed that cup of hot tea to calm down and do some serious thinking. The owner was an old man, and he asked me, "Are you getting drafted to join the army and going to war?" "You seem worried." I told him, "Yes, I am worried, but we have to serve our country and be brave. I didn't want the old man to doubt me and had to make sure he was not going to tell me I couldn't trust anyone these days, not even my own people. Many of them work with the secret service, and they are willing to do anything for money, so this old man is not an exception, even though he sounds very sincere. "You have an accent. Are you Kurdish? Yes, I am." Then he replied, "Please be careful. Just because you are Kurdish, the government will put you on the front line so you can die faster. And either way, they will win because there will be fewer Kurdish people to worry about. I thanked the old man and kept the conversation short. I just wasn't in a good mood to carry on any conversation at this time. Deep down inside, I knew I couldn't serve this government; and I kept repeating to myself, "Yes, I must find a way to leave this country, to live a good life and enjoy freedom." I knew there would be a price to pay, and that there would be suffering and a long journey to a brighter future. I went home and told my family what had happened. They felt good about my decision, and we discussed how to get me out of the country as soon as possible. We all knew if

I got caught by the local police and security service that works undercover for the government, they would definitely either kill me or hang me by the neck. You always have to be on your toes. Police are everywhere, and they will often jail Kurdish people for doing nothing or just getting someone to snitch on you. I am not going to join the army to defend a racist government that doesn't give us any rights. I kept a low profile and stayed home. And on occasions, I spent some time with a few of my friends that I trusted. The consequence of refusal to get drafted is absolute death, and you will have to be prepared to not surrender or give in. For the next nine months, I lived in fear and, in the meantime, the war was getting longer and bloodier. People were getting killed by the hour, and one could hear people losing their loved ones every day. In fact, two of my cousins were among the people who were killed during the first year of the war. There was no way out of this war. The government was desperate for more money and more people to get to war. They were asking all people to give up their jewelry, gold, and as much money as they can to be donated to the holy war, a nonsense war without merit or meaning. People don't even know how the war started and what caused it. All one could see on TV and hear on the radio was talk about the courageous leader and how wonderful he is and that we should all go to war because "It's a Holy War." The poor people of this country knew that this was all about Saddam Hussein; they were there just to make him look good, and he could care less about people. He was no hero, and everything we saw and heard was not true. There was so much fear and intimidation everyone had to praise and pretend to love the leader and be willing to die for him. Nobody could ever say anything bad about him, only good things. A friend of mine stepped on an old newspaper with Saddam Hussein's picture on it by mistake, and he was beaten severely by a couple of police officers. They did not stop until he picked up the newspaper and kissed the picture, and apologized. There are police and secret police everywhere and watching every step we make, every move we take. You always have to watch over your shoulder a brutal regime with no mercy and compassion for its own people. You have to be one of them. You have to sell yourself and betray your own people. Innocent people were being put in jail and tortured. The government wanted to send a clear and precise message that you were either with us or against us. This was the kind of regime that we had to deal with. Out of fear, people were marching in the street, praising the leader carrying his picture and shouting, "For you, we will die; for you, we will give everything we have".

Being 'Kurdish' meant we would always be considered a 'second class citizen.' The treacherous Baathist party of the Iraqi government wanted and was still trying to remove the people of Kurdistan from their land. They drove us out our villages and towns, and they burned our land and farm. No wonder the majority of Kurdish people refused to be expelled from the land of their ancestors, and they took up arms against the government. I convinced myself that I would not serve this regime, even if my life depended on it... I would find a way to be free, and even if I didn't make it out, the fight would be worth it. I decided to go into hiding and get myself out of this country. I knew I had the courage and the commitment to do something about it, and that's where my plan started... I knew that I had to keep a low profile and stay with family and a few trusted friends. Deserting the army and refusing to get drafted is a huge deal, and the punishment is death. I knew I was taking a huge risk, but I also knew this was the only way "I will not serve a regime that does not recognize my rights. I will not be part of this bloody war that is causing hundreds of people to die every day on the battlefield with no reason whatsoever and all of that so our goddamn president can look good" this thought occupied my mind for hours and hours, and I know the risk will be great but knowing how good I felt by not being part of the regime. I needed to have a solid plan that could allow me to stay safe and keep a low profile while I worked on a plan to get out of the country. As the days were getting longer, I knew it was a matter of time before I would get caught if I didn't get some new identification. Everywhere you go in Iraq, there are checkpoints at the corner of the city. The police are everywhere, always looking for those who deserted the army and those who refuse to be drafted, they can come up to you anytime and ask you for your identification, and since my identification shows that I was supposed to be drafted, I had to find ways to fake an identification, and of course, with money, you can bribe anyone and everyone. Lucky for me, I took my brother's identification, who's 3 years younger than I am, which is easily convincing somehow since we look alike. I took my brother's identification to one of my closest friends, had his photo removed, and inserted mine with a special technique that he used without damaging the documents. With some extra cash, he took it to the office where all passports and documents were processed and got stamped and processed with my photo on the same day. This identification showed me three years younger with my brother's name. There were only a handful of people I could trust. In fact, only a few of my friends knew that I was using fake identification, and I convinced the majority of my other friends that I was still in school and had one more year to get drafted. I spent most of my time hiding and reading books. I knew if I got caught, it would be the end of me because one has no rights in the Iraqi jail. I would get beaten so badly that I would rather die than go to jail. That was my plan. I even bought a small handgun to carry with me sometimes, but not while I was in the city because I could always use my new identification to get around. It's not easy being a Kurdish citizen in the country of Iraq. A lot of pressure was on us from everywhere, the pressure of dealing with a regime that doesn't accept your language and doesn't recognize your right. In order to get anywhere, you have to pretend that you are not Kurdish. I still managed to travel and even get together with some friends while my Mom and Dad were working on a plan to get me out of the country through Northern Iraq, where Kurdish people live. Everything was controlled by the Iraqi regime, with the exception of the mountains, where a majority of Kurdish fighters were hiding. So my goal was to get to the Kurdish fighter. However, traveling from one city to another was not easy, and you had to go through numerous checkpoints. These checkpoints were so intimidating, fear was evident, and you had to go through at least 3 to 4 checkpoints that were so intense. You could see some of these security personnel carrying huge sticks in their hands, similar to police batons, and they were ready to wipe and hit anyone who seemed to be suspicious or nervous. It seems impossible to get through some of these checkpoints unless you know someone or have valid identification.

Planning to get out of the city in the most careful way and taking all kinds of precautions to make sure, first of all, that I had the right identification. Her number one priority was working, finding, and having an identity that looked legit so that it would be easy for me to go through a checkpoint.

The City of Mosul, where I lived until I left Iraq, was beautiful. It was located in Northern Iraq, approximately 250 miles Northwest of Baghdad. The original city stands on the West Bank of the Tigris River. On the opposite side, which is the east bank, is the ancient City of Nineveh, one of the oldest cities in Iraq, where the majority of Kurdish people live. The city of Mosul has many nice places to see and enjoy, e.g., several theaters, nightclubs, and bars. At the time when I was there, numerous tourists were visiting the city. And as a tour guide, I was able to perfect my English, and several times, I invited some of the tourists to my house to stay free of charge. And they enjoyed our hospitality. Despite the fear that we lived in, I knew in my heart that I would miss the city of Mosul after I had left. Today, the city of Mosul has changed and got destroyed between the war in Iraq and Iran in the '80s, which lasted 8 years and Isis controlling the city in 2014. They imposed hard rules on the city and destroyed all monuments, historical and valuable monuments, and they burnt all churches, mosques all by the name of Islam. Islam has nothing to do with violence. Just like any religion, they promote peace and prosperity and allow everyone to live peacefully together. Isis committed genocide toward the Yazidi minority. After the allied forces(American, Kurdish and Iraqi forces) drove ISIS out of the city, the city of Mosul was ruined. Today, the city of Mosul is nothing like it was in the '70s and '80s. It is getting rebuilt but it'll be a long time before the city rises up. I'm sure it will.

Meanwhile, the war was getting longer and bloodier during the first year 1980. Both the Iraq and Iran governments were deploying more troops to the front line and they were bombarding cities on both sides with jet fighters destroying everything. There was no limit on their target. A lot of civilians were getting killed from both sides. Furthermore, the Iraqi government we're getting desperate, and they were recruiting people and calling all the reserves to join the battlefield. They were always looking for more young people to ship to the warzone, and they also knew there were people who abandoned their post and those like me, who refused to get drafted and join their war, which was nothing less than a matter of pride to the president who cared less about his nation and people, the only thing you can see is Saddam Huessin all over the news all over the city, his picture of carrying a sword aiming toward great victory, great honour and his courageous journey toward defeating the enemy. There were images of him everywhere and anywhere. All you could see on our TV were things about him touring the warzone and shaking soldiers' hands, kissing them on the cheek, and thanking them, which were lies. He just wanted people to remember that he's at the battlefield, but in reality, he was hiding in a bunker. People were sick of the war, especially seeing the damage the war is bringing to them, and seeing their loved ones getting killed. In the meanwhile, our city was getting bombed by Iranian jet fighters. They were bombing the city every day, and it was getting destroyed, and people were getting killed and buried in their homes.

I remember the Iraqi government officials notifying people about their loved ones being killed in the warzone, and they told people that their loved ones were considered martyrs, and that they were killed for the cause of God and the country's defense. People will be getting these coffins wrapped up in the Iraqi flag, and families were not allowed to see if the coffin had their loved one inside.

Teenagers were getting shipped to the warzone every day, and God forbid. If anyone got caught with fake identification, it would be the end. There was no such thing as your rights or your opinion. The law, "you are innocent until proven guilty," does not exist here since all judges and lawyers are appointed by the government. Even the lawyer that you get to help you out works for the government as well. The city was tightly patrolled, and the policemen and the secret security police were on every corner checking on people, especially those that deserted the military. On a cool evening night, one of my friends insisted that I go and see a movie with him. He assured me there would be no patrol and we'll only be gone for 2 hours. After putting a lot of thought into it, I decided to go and see a movie. Western movies and all-American movies were a must-watch for me. Movies such as, "Rebel Without a Cause", "West Side Story," and "High Noon with Gary Cooper," are movies that I must have watched many times, and that's how I learned my English by watching movies over and over again. Today, I still enjoy watching these movies all the time.

After some thought, we decided to go ahead to the movie theaters. I took my identification, and we were ready to purchase the tickets to see a movie. There were hundreds of people purchasing tickets. I waited for almost 15 minutes.

People enjyed going to the theater just to get out and forget about the war that was taking a heavy toll on everyone and anyone. People were tired and exhausted. We enjoyed the movie even though I was always looking over my shoulder just to make sure I was safe. Little did I know that the police and the secret security service, who were dressed up in civilian uniforms, were waiting outside the theater, looking for people who deserted the military service and those who refused to get drafted, people like me. We found out after leaving the theater that there was a long line, and they were checking everyone's identification. I was very nervous and started to panic. My friend was trying hard to calm me down, and I knew I had no choice but to calm down. The feeling of getting caught was unbearable. There was this police officer with a long stick in his hand, ready to beat anyone they could find with no identification. Just before our turn for the post, someone turned up out of the crowd who was so nervous and shaking. They knew there was something wrong with him, and when they found out, they started striking him with the stick. They shoved him down to a patrol car, and that guy was praying for mercy. I'm begging the the policeman to stop. He was covering his face and head, bleeding all over. I stood out there with my legs shaking and my heart beating fast, not knowing what was going to happen? When my turn came, close to the end of the line, they just looked at me, and one of the guys asked, "How was the movie?" I answered him, "Ok". Then he said, "Go ahead." That was one terrifying moment that I experienced.

That day, I went home and promised myself I would keep it low. The days were getting longer, and sooner or later, I knew I had to find a way to get out. Most of the time, I just stayed home reading books. That was my refuge, and I swear I felt good by reading constantly.

The second terrifying experience occurred when I was shopping at a second-hand store. I was wearing a nice used shirt with some stickers, and I believe there was a Texas flag on the side, which was very naive on my part, especially knowing that I was in hiding and using my brother's identification. I was taken by two secret service men who were very rough with their questioning, and they started to accuse me of being an American spy. They started to push me, and one of them pulled the sticker off my shirt and tore it while the other man pulled my hair which was a little longer, and started questioning me, "What's with the long hair?". I was dragged, kicked, and beaten with a baton.mOne of the guys left to get the patrol car. I was left alone with the other guy who was holding my hand and had me down with his foot on my neck, where I was having an extremely hard time breathing. I knew this was the end, and I had to do something really fast. So I had one or two choices -- keep my mouth shut and let them take me to jail, hoping I would be released, or go with my second option, to free myself from him and run. I knew I had to do something fast and wanted to go with the second option. So I asked the guy to please let me get up. He had his knee on my neck. I begged him because I could not breathe, he pulled me from my shirt and I stood up, and he kicked me in my side. I got up really fast and grabbed his shirt, and with as much power as I could, I hit him with my head and broke his nose, then he immediately passed out. I felt really good, especially knowing that he was down. I ran as fast as I could, and I was still soaked with blood from his broken nose and my blood from getting beaten up. I got to a big store and decided to hide for a few hours. I could hear more patrol cars looking for me. At this point, and later in the evening after I got home, I knew that I had to get out of the country fast. And I was also afraid that someone would report me to the authorities. I had to develop a game plan soon.

Months went by, and my living situation was getting harder and harder. Living with the fear of getting caught, I'm constantly alert. I mostly kept a low profile and tried to stay home as much as I could. I kept pressuring my family to find a way to give me out, they were working very hard on it, and I knew sooner or later, I had to get out. There are only so many people you can trust, and before someone snitched on me and put an end to my hiding, I knew it was time. I also knew that I had to wait and be patient.

The situation in the war was getting bloodier, and the government was getting more desperate to recruit more people to deploy to the war zone. I remember hearing about so many people who got killed in the war zone in our neighborhood, yet the government of Iraq, Saddam Hussein's regime, continued to celebrate their fake victory and they were assuring people that they had the upper hand. Our people could not keep money in the bank. They were afraid the government would take it by the name of Jihad, and there was a shortage of food and supplies throughout the market. People were panic buying and emptying all the shelves. It was a rough time for all of us.

CHAPTER TWO

In Late August 1981, I finally had the green light to leave. A very close family friend came down to take me to Northern Iraqi Kurdistan, the land of Kurds where the majority of Kurdish people live. This is our region in northern Iraq, where Kurds are the majority ethnic group.

I knew we had to go through some serious checkpoints. There were checkpoints everywhere in Iraq. To travel from one city to another, we would typically go through a few checkpoints, and during any of these checkpoints, the government's tactic was to use fear and intimidation against us. I knew I had to calm down, especially since I would be using my brother's identification with his name and my photo on the ID. I also advised the person with me not to call me by my name but by my brother's name, which is 'Jaffar,' an Arabic name that should make things easy at the checkpoints. Also, being fluent in both Arabic and my native language Kurdish, was very helpful to me. Most Kurdish people speak Arabic but not very well. Growing up in the City of Mosul, which was dominated by Arabs, and my friends were both Kurdish and Arabs, as well as the Arabic school I attended, gave me a strong background in both Kurdish and Arabic languages. I'm ready and willing to do whatever it takes to make the journey. The journey which will define and shape my future. There's no future living here and being abused and harassed constantly. I knew in my heart that my journey wasn't going to be easy, but I also knew I had to be strong that day. I cut my hair and made sure the clothes I was wearing would not draw any attention at the checkpoint. I kept things simple. My mom told me, "You will be fine, son. I have been praying for you every day." It was hard to leave my family and friends, especially my mother. But I knew I had to leave fast. I had the opportunity to say goodbye to my family but not to some of my closest friends. There was no time. I wish I had the time to say goodbye to my friends, especially those that knew about my situation and who were very loyal to me. However, I told my brother to say goodbye on my behalf. Early in the morning on the following day, we got into the car and left for the bus station. The plan was to travel north to the city called Duhok City, which is inhabited by predominantly Kurdish people. The city was about an hour's drive from Mosul, encircled by mountains along the Tigris river. The bus we took was old, and it was packed with people and their belongings. This was going to be one long journey. My heart was pounding. I was scared, and my anxiety level was uncontrollable. I kept trying to put on a smiley face and pretending everything was going to be great. When we arrived at the first checkpoint, we were all asked to get off the bus and line up. We all lined up with our identifications. The police officer was checking through all IDs, and when he came to check mine, he looked at me and said, "Why are you traveling up north"? I answered by saying that I was visiting family members. I was trying hard to control my fear and emotions. He suddenly said, "Ok go ahead." What a relief! However, we had to go through another checkpoint before we reached the city. At the next checkpoint, there were more police officers checking people as we stood in line, waiting for our turn. I saw one of the police beating one of the passengers and pushing him to another car. I started to panic and wanted to get out of sight. This was a very tense moment, and out of nowhere, as I was getting closer to showing my identification to the police officer, I heard my name. It was one of the officers who went to school with me for many years. He was one of those guys who liked everything about me since I was so popular at school. He always wanted to be my friend. I was very popular in high school, and a lot of kids thought I was cool because I spoke English well and knew a lot about the

USA and Western movies. Anything has to do with western culture. I was very good at it, and that's one of the many reasons people at school wanted to get close to me and be my friend. At one point, I used to dress up like John Travolta in the movie "Saturday Night Fever." I bought a similar suit from a second-hand store just like his and even learned how to dance like him. As he approached me, he shook my hand and gave me a big hug, followed by a kiss on each cheek.

Suddenly I was sweaty, and my heart was pounding fast. I tried to take a deep breath to calm myself down, but my breathing was so sharp, and it was noticeable that I was having sudden episodes of anxiety attacks. The guy continued to grab my hand and give me another hug, followed by one more kiss on each cheek.

This is a Middle Eastern tradition- to kiss on the cheek. I was very nervous because my identification was my brother's name, not mine, and he called me by my name. I knew I was busted, but luckily, he said, "I don't need to see your papers. I know you." I started to breathe easier and got on the bus again. My family's friend who was with me said, "Are you ready for one more checkpoint?" I thought he was kidding, but he said there was one more, and this one was not as strict. There is only one officer, and most of the time, he will just let you pass. As we approached the checkpoint, the officer just waved at us, and we finally arrived in the city after two hours which should have been one hour. But all the checkpoints and the delay made it long. This was one of the longest rides through my journey, knowing if I got caught with fake identification, it would be the end. When we arrived in the City of Duhok, I took a deep breath with not much strength left in me. Even though I knew we were not 100% out of the danger zone yet, but it sure felt pretty good being around Kurdish people.

Duhok City is predominantly populated by Kurdish people. The city is encircled by mountains along the Tigris river and is located in the northern part of Iraq.

We stopped at my uncle's house for some food and shelter for the day because there was another long road ahead of us, and this one required us to go through some alternative road to make it to rebel's base. The following morning we boarded an old truck with my guide, and we drove toward the mountains on a very narrow dirt road. It took us almost an hour to get to a little village, where I was dropped off by myself with nothing but a small backpack. I was told to stay and wait and keep a low profile. Someone would be there to pick me up shortly.

The area where I waited was beautiful. There was a long valley surrounded by high mountains. I could hear birds singing and water streaming from a narrow waterfall hitting the bottom of the valley. I felt that I was the only one there. After I had waited for more than two hours, I started to wonder if this guy was going to show up. While I was thinking about all this, an older man showed up carrying a long German rifle. He was also loaded with ammunition all over his body, and he looked as if he was ready to go to war. His eyes were sharp, indicating the hardship of the road. He approached me with a deep voice, "Are you ready?" I answered, "Yes, sir." Then he asked me, "Do you know who I am?" "No, sir. I don't know who you are." He said, "I am your uncle." He handed me a pistol and asked me if I knew how to use it, just in case. I told him I could handle the gun, "Very well," he said. "Let's move." We had a long road ahead of us, and there were other people who were waiting to be picked up. We set out on a narrow dirt road and traveled through some very rough mountain terrain. We continued to follow the path through a valley and on the edge of a small river that flows through this valley. I believe we walked for at least three to four hours before we even sat down and took a break. My uncle kept me on the run. I kept saying to myself, "This man is very strong. How is he able to walk for such a long time without breaking a sweat?" He must be, at least, in his late fifties. He looked old but strong. The living situation for these comrades was very hard. They are always on the run and always in fear of the enemy, they live off of the land, and they travel from one village to another village carrying their belongings and their guns. I kindly asked him him for food and time to rest for a bit, but all he had was some dry bread and water, which was more than enough to satisfy our need for food and water. As we got close to a small village, I was really excited knowing that we were going to have a nice hot meal. We arrived at the village, and had a nice warm meal and water that was offered to us by one of the villagers. Best meal in a long time, and now we needed to rest. I was hoping my uncle will allow us to stay for the night. After all, we are exhausted, or rather, I am exhausted. I was in desperate need for some sleep. My uncle told me we would be spending the night at the village with top-notch hospitality. They took excellent care of us, and I made sure to keep my stomach full.

After a long walk, I had no problem falling asleep and slept throughout the night. On the following day, right at dawn, we had breakfast and hot tea. We were able to get some extra bread for the road. I felt that I was ready to continue the journey, so we left the village. With an unknown destination, we walked for several hours. I was informed by my uncle that we will be picking up more guys who have been waiting for him. We reached our destination. There were over 15 people waiting, including families and kids. We started our journey with our guide, which is my uncle, who had very little patience for crying kids. He made it very clear to us that we had to control our kids and keep the noise down, especially when we arrived at the camp where the soldiers were stationed at the top of the mountain. We traveled through the valley, which was close to the camp (of the enemy). That was the only safe way to get through. Our guide kept telling us to keep quiet and to stay together throughout the journey. He placed a lot of fear in all of us, but then again, he was the expert, and he knew the situation better than we did.

We started our journey. I was one of the people who stayed in the rear, helping a family who had younger kids. Our dirt road was surrounded by a lot of big trees. These trees gave us shade and made the trip a little easier. In fact, we enjoyed eating a lot of wild fruits as we traveled on our journey. We arrived at yet, another village where we spent a few hours and got plenty of rest. At midnight, the guide came and gathered all of us. He explained to us what we needed to do as we crossed to our next point, we had to go through this deep valley, and this valley is surrounded by an Iraqi camp at the top of the hill. We can only cross in the night during the day time. This will be our only way out. Keep in mind that if we get caught, that will be our end. "We will do this, one group at a time". He also advised us that the family with kids is to make sure that they are asleep and have their hand on their mouth in case they cry to keep them quiet. As we got closer to the valley that would take us to the Kurdish fighters, we had to make sure the kids were asleep. I was one of the first ones to go through carrying one of the kids in my arms; luckily, it was a small kid. I walked very slowly, holding my breath. I could even hear some of the soldiers talking and joking. In-fact, I heard one of the soldiers say, "I think I hear somebody walking through the bushes." But one of the other soldiers said, "I think it's only your imagination. Let's get to the camp before we get trapped by Kurdish rebels." I finally made it through with the kid still sleeping in my arms. I sat down, breathing a little easier, and waited for the rest, hoping they would all make it safely, and we all did. This was one nerve-racking journey that I will not forget. It felt like an eternity knowing how close we came to the enemy carrying little kids with us. Our guide continued to push us to walk more. He just wanted to make sure we were in a safe zone away from the enemy line. Despite how exhausted we were, we all knew that he was doing the right thing. A few more miles was not going to hurt. After all, we were almost there. He kept encouraging us and assuring us it was just a matter of time. As we got close after a few hours of walking, we found a spot tucked in at the end of the valley. Our guys pointed at that spot and said this is where we are going to rest. It was a pretty good spot at the end of the valley, overlooking an open land. We spend the few hours that were left in the night resting in the open land. This is the end of summer. We are approaching the autumn season, where it gets extremely cold at night and hot during the daytime. With not much clothes on during the cold night. I sensed that we were all so tired we just fell asleep.

As the morning sun was getting stronger and brighter, we hit the trail again. Climbing up the mountains and going down into the valleys, we had some members of our group who decided to stay behind and go back to a nearby village and then go back to the city. Some of the people that went back had some health conditions such as diabetes and heart disorder, constant hunger and thirst as well as the long walk made it hard for them. For me, there was no going back. I'm going to continue walking until I get to my destination. We kept going and going until I felt the bottom of my foot getting as hard as a rock with a blister right in the middle, which made it extremely hard for me to walk. The shoes I was wearing weren't designed for walking. I stopped for a moment and wrapped my foot up with a piece of an old t-shirt that I had. At that point, it made it much easier for me to walk. After a brutal few miles of walking, we reached the next village which belonged to Kurdish people. The village was almost completely destroyed few home were still standing, which allowed the villagers to stay and rebuild. The government and their jet fighters destroyed most of the villages. Destroyed all mosques and churches and water supplies.

As the sun sat on the top of the mountains, I saw freedom. I saw my life changing and I felt good. I felt free and not stripped of our rights as Kurdish people who had been living under the dictatorship of the Iraqi leader, Saddam, the unjust government who would do anything and everything to destroy any Kurdish person who joined the Kurdish revolutionaries. The people in the village were very generous with what little they had. Looking at their children, looking at their sad smiles, wondering what happened? Where's their laughter? Their smile? Their eyes tell a sad, tearful story. We all want to make the children laugh by sharing some good funny stories with them. People in the village were very nice, and they shared everything with us and supplied us with all the goods we needed to make it through our journey. As the night sank into darkness, we fell asleep for a very long time, and it was as if nothing could wake us up, then we heard our guide asking us to wake up because we had to leave soon. Those people who decided to leave us and return back home had reported us to the government. And now the government was looking for us. We had to leave that village immediately so we would not put those people in that village at risk. We packed up fast and thanked the people at the village, gave them some money, and purchased a couple of mules from them to carry the kids and some of the supplies, and we took off as fast as we could.

As we were traveling toward the mountains, we heard helicopters flying toward the village and the mountains. The helicopter crew started shooting at us. We hid underneath the rocks and the trees to escape the shooting. A couple of our people shot back at the helicopter and put in a good fight. But we were no match for the helicopter's guns. We had to spread out through the rockiest mountains and stay down, and as we approached the night, the helicopter left. We gathered our team to evaluate the situation. Even though we were exhausted and tired, we moved slowly towards the mountains. We didn't camp until it was close to dawn. When we decided to rest, it wasn't long before the guide asked us to wrap up and get ready. It's time to move again. We got some dry bread and water to eat, and also, there were a lot of wild fruits that we ate throughout our journey. Every time I sat down to rest, I thought about my family, wondering how everyone was doing. Are they under pressure from the government? Typically, once the authority finds out that one person is missing and not in the military, then they start harassing the family about where they are and how come they are not home. My mom and dad were advised if that ever happened, they needed to not give any information and to pretend that they had nothing to do with my disappearance and not being on the battlefield against the enemy. My family was advised what to tell the government official in case they ever asked "Where is your son, Waleed?"

They knew that their answer would be, "If it's up to us, my son will be fighting our enemy, not running away. We have nothing to do with him. We are ashamed".

You do not have much choice but to say that. The government will kill anyone and everyone, regardless of how old you are, if you do not agree with them.

If it's up to them, they should be serving. The consequences of their involvement in helping their son will be imprisonment. I felt good knowing that they were prepared to deal with this. I still worry about them and hope they will be safe.

With all these thoughts, I couldn't rest, even though I was exhausted. The government of Saddam Hussein was brutal, and their tactic was "torture." So many of my friends from school were put away for days just for saying the wrong thing or for not agreeing with the regime. You learn to praise the goverment at all the time and must be willing to do whatever it takes to be ready to serve. We were advised to fight to the end if we ever got to a situation close to getting captured. We would rather die while fighting than give ourselves up. You will get tortured, and in some cases, one of the comrades showed us all the bruises throughout his body. He showed his hand where they even pulled some of his nails. He was set free because they didn't find anything on him. To me, that was enough to feel so good about refusing to get drafted. I didn't feel guilty. In fact, I felt great.

These mountains, hills, and valleys belong to this Kurdish people. This is where ancestry lived this land for hundreds of years, it is our land, and we will fight for it.

We set off, with our torn-up feet leading us through a bumpy road that slopes down from the top of the mountain to the deep valley. The day was in distress as the heat from the sun burned my face, but we continued the path across the mountains through the valley's ups and downs, with no signs of our guide giving us a break to rest. As the sun started to fade behind the mountains, the cool breeze moved in, and we were in no shape to continue moving. We begged our guide to let us rest more. I think he felt for us because we had kids with us and we sat down to rest near an abandoned mill for no more than one hour. Our guide person nicely explained to us that we had only a few more miles to get to the next village and it would be good when we got there because we needed the rest. Thank God for the two mules we brought with us. They helped, especially with the kids.

CHAPTER THREE

This next village was absolutely beautiful, surrounded by thick trees and tucked at the age of the mountains. Everything here is so peaceful and quiet besides the soft sounds of birds and the sound of watery murmur dressed in the rocks superimposed on the edge of the mountains. It's nice to feel the shadow from the trees keep us nice and cool. I have never seen anything so calm and quiet. This village belonged to the Kurdish rebels who treated us like heroes. We had a nice meal, and we rested under the shade of the trees until we were told that there would be a group of Kurdish fighters who'll take us to the Kurdish base right by the border of Turkey. We needed the rest, but I couldn't wait to meet some of these brave fighters that protected Kurdish land and the people who lived in it. The only way for any Iraqi soldiers to get here was by helicopter or a jet fighter. This was Kurdish land. Years back, this was a beautiful land until the Iraqi Government destroyed everything to the point that it was impossible to live on the land, but we are strong, and we will build it again. With this land that has rich and great soil, little by little, it will prosper, and people will live free. It has been our dream to live in our land and speak our own language without fear and intimidation. We will prevail, and we will live free. After all, it's our land, and our people deserve to be free. Kurdish people who live in Turkey, Iran, and Syria are in the same situation. They live in fear, and they are abused by their regime. We, the Kurdish people, like to live like any other nation. We like to have our freedom, we want to be able to speak our own language without the fear of using our own language, and we like to live in our land peacefully and be part of the world community.

After a long wait, the group of Kurdish fighters showed up to take us to the Kurdish base, they had all kinds of weapons, and they were ready to put out the fight if needed. We were so happy to see them. Their leader said we had to keep everything secret. "We can't tell you where our next move is or which way we will be going and for yours and our protection, but we will be moving to the base, and it's going to be a very rough road." "You will be facing some of the most challenging mountains. You need to pay attention to our instruction. It will be a long way," he pointed at the top of the mountain, which I thought there was no end to it and it was covered with thick fog so we couldn't see that top of the mountain. We all understood what he meant and got ready to hit the road. In order for us to leave Northern Iraq to go to Iran as refugees, we had to go through some parts of Turkey and back and forth from the North of Iraq and South of Turkey and on the border since we could not get to Turkey. If we get caught by the Turkish forces, that will be another big problem. They will probably either put us in jail or surrender us to the Iraqi regime. Either way, it wasn't easy. We had only one choice, and that was to cross the border cautiously. Be on alert throughout the the crossing process. Some of the roads are so narrow and so sharp, sharp rocks everywhere, which were good to hide in case of a helicopter attack on us. Here we are surrounded by the enemy from all borders. The people on the Turkish side were mostly Kurdish from Turkey. Kurdish people in Turkey, are under the same abuse we are going through, brutal government that was well known to destroy anything that's Kurdish. We were all in the same boat. Whether you were Kurdish from Iraq, Turkey, Iran, or Syria, you had no rights and were always considered to be a second citizen. Kurdish in Turkey sympathized with us because they felt our pain and suffering. They helped us with food and supplies. We also didn't impose on them; we were quick in and out as we crossed the border. Our Kurdish fighters knew what it meant to be strong and ready to tackle whatever got in your way. I felt ready to move and make a difference, knowing what I had to go through for the past few months. Living under fear, it was time for me to make my journey, and whatever happened, I would be free. I don't care if I die of hunger or thirst. I will at least be free.

We started to move towards the mountains through a narrow valley, rocks everywhere, big and small rocks covering the edge of the mountains. The surrounding mountains seemed like they were hanging from the sky. To me, it felt like it was impossible to climb up these mountains. The experienced guys were telling us, "No worries, we will go through it." As the cool breeze faded and the heat from the sun got brighter, we slowly started to move toward the impossible mountains. Our legs were getting tired, but we kept moving and moving. And every time we stopped to rest we enjoyed each other's company. Water and bread were all that we have in our backpack. We also managed to carry a small teapot to make hot tea, which is a must in Iraq. Everybody drinks hot tea with lots of sugar regardless of how hot the weather is. The Iraqi people enjoy smoking and drinking hot tea. Every time we sit down, we take out our teapot and get the wood to make the fire. The tea just tasted really good. One of the guys started to tell us about how he makes a delicious tea and the secret of making an excellent cup of hot tea and he went on by explaining, "You must bring the water to a boil first, then add tea leaves and leave it to simmer for a few minutes, then enjoy a nice cup of hot tea." I guess we had time on our hands, so the conversation went about the secret of making an excellent cup of hot tea, then it moved up to different subjects and more stories about the war.

All I kept thinking about was how much longer before we would get to the Kurdish base. I think we walked through some of the roughest roads where there was nothing to see except burned villages and forests destroyed by Iraqi jet fighters. We did see a few wild dogs looking for food. The Iraqi government has burned most of the natural resources that people depend on. They made it very hard for anyone to live here except the nomads who traveled from one area to another. This was a beautiful land at one point. The land was full of life and happy people. The old man started to tear up, and he was showing signs of sadness and sorrow. He raised his head up and started to talk about the comrades who were martyred as they were defending their land. As he described his days when he was young and lived with his family. He looked at us as he drank his cup of tea with a cigarette in his mouth. He had some sad stories, and as the evening moved on and the wind became stronger and cooler, he laid his head down, touching the ground, and said, "We lost our whole village and several members of my family."

He continued telling us his sad story and how the village was attacked and people left dead, "We fought with what we had, but we were no match to their helicopter and jet fighter. Everything got burned and destroyed, and when the soldiers came, they burned everything. Bodies of the villagers were lying out there. We went back to bury them. Killing innocent people, kids, and women with no mercy," struggling to hold his cup of tea, he teared up and said, "They are all in heaven. These people died for no reason".

Every story was revealed to the group. It was a sad one. Every one of us had a story of torture and fear to tell and share. Kurdish people suffered and still suffering all over. Whether are Kurdish from Iraq, Iran, Turkey, or Syria, we are surrounded by killers regimes that hated Kurdish people. After World War 1, Western powers promised Kurdish their own homeland in the agreement known as the Treaty of Servers. But a later agreement instead divided them among Turkey, Iraq, Syria, and Iran. Today there are about 30 million Kurds living across the region, with about half in Turkey.

Our hope is to have our own country and land where we can be free and where I can tell people I'm from Kurdistan(Kurd Land). That sure feels good.

We spent the night thinking about the poor old man and everything that had happened here, and we all gathered around the wood fire. The breeze was getting cooler as we slipped into the depth of the night.

The morning sun moved up, and we were all ready to continue our journey. I felt pretty good and well-rested, and so did the rest of our team. The path we traveled was a narrow dirt road, so we had to split into smaller groups of ten people rather than the large group of 100 people. The smaller groups were easier to hide from the enemy. In the makeup of the groups, families were kept together as much as possible because the children walked slower or had to be carried on the shoulders of the parents or placed on mules. Thank God for our Kurdish fighters who were guiding us. They were so brave and patient, guiding a bunch of city slickers across the mountains. I admired their courage and their level of commitment every step of the way. They were there to protect and guide us, and we were very grateful.

We kept walking, and all I could see was huge land that never seemed to have an ending. We continued on our path, not stopping until we reached another village which had been destroyed by the Iraqi government, but people still lived there. They had managed to build a few homes, establish several farms and produce some livestock to keep them sustained. They welcomed us with open arms and offered us food. We shared the food between the families, and before we went to sleep, we were asked to take turns patrolling the village, which meant you had to be at the entrance of the village watching for any unusual activities. My turn was at midnight. I was handed a rifle and asked to monitor and guard the entrance of the village for anything suspicious. I was by myself for the whole hour watching my team. I felt like a prison guard and stayed awake until my relief came in and took over.

The morning sun moved in slowly, and I woke up in a perfect place. This was the same place I saw yesterday, but it looked more open and beautiful and surrounded by large trees everywhere, which made it easier to tolerate the heat during the long summer days, which can get very hot and it can reach over 100 degrees. This village was right on the corner of a tiny river, and the house we stayed in stood right by that river. It had an old broken fence surrounded by what seemed to be an oak tree. I wish we could stay for a little longer and rest more so we could have more energy, but we got to be on the run throughout the whole trip.

"It's time to move," shouted the old man. We gathered all of our belongings, and I made sure there was plenty of tea and bread for the road. We set out down the road once again, and this road was narrow and extremely rocky around the edge of the valley. We had to climb up one of the rockiest mountains. It was even hard for the two mules to move with all the supplies they were carrying. We had to unload all supplies and pull the mules up. When we made it to the top of the mountains, we were exhausted. It wasn't easy, especially having younger kids with us. I was very hungry and thirsty, so we were in no position to move anymore. Between hunger and thirst and crying kids, we finally took some time to rest and build a little fire. It felt good taking a break and enjoy whatever food we have. With the small amount of food and water, I managed to boil some water in my stained teapot. We sat down and shared the bread and passed the water around. I didn't think I could continue to walk. My legs were tired, and we were ready for a nap. I believe we rested for approximately one hour, which seemed like a few minutes, and I felt no strength in my legs with a little stretching. I was able to gain strength. We were ordered to get ready and get moving again. Hit the road again! This time we had to climb very steep mountains and our guide kept telling us we were almost there, don't give up. And we didn't. We all stuck together like a team, and we finally got to the Kurdish fighters base. "The rebel base," where the Kurdish fighter operated and made their move, was a place that seemed to be hanging at the edge of the mountains. And from far away, as we were approaching, the place looked hidden between the high mountains with only a few tents and half-built homes that were destroyed by jet fighters. We understood from the fighters that they had to hide their base because of the Iraqi soldiers and their fighters. To me, this was a turning point. Here I *am in my freedom land, surrounded by my people*. I'm happy despite what we have been through for the last few days. We stayed at the base for a few days, and we had plenty of rest. I particularly enjoyed staying at the Kurdish fighters base. Not only we got plenty of food to eat, but we also enjoyed the many friends we meet during our stay. The nights were magical, especially watching the shining stars in the sky. They were so close and bright that it felt like I could touch the stars. I have never seen anything like this. The cool breeze from the mountains was cold, and it seemed winter season was on the horizon. Daytime was a different story, where the sun was warm and bright. Well rested with not much to do besides a few hours of daily training on weapon use and survival for our upcoming journey. Often times I wandered around the camp, keeping myself occupied during the day, and on cool nights, we sat around the fire to keep warm and listen to our comrades sharing their stories of courage and their life experience and what they have gone through to be a step ahead the brutal and unjust regime of the government.

It takes courage and commitment to be here. These revolutionary Kurdish people are in their land protecting what belongs to them, and no matter what it takes, they're committed to carry on and stand in the face of the government

"Isn't it better to die here in these beautiful mountains defending your land?" that thought came to me every time I felt discouraged. Truly makes sense to me. I would rather be here than be their soldier and get killed for a regime that doesn't believe in our rights. I'm convinced that my journey here will lead to better and brighter future. After we met with the revolutionary leaders and got some insight on what was next for us, the plan was to stay another week and wait for more people to join us before we continued our journey. This trip would be a long one. We stayed and enjoyed the hospitality of the (focus). And they went out of their way to make us feel welcome.

We sat down with our team to discuss our journey. There were a few comrades who were assigned to accompany us on the journey, they knew the way, and they had been through the journey many times. They will also be well-equipped with small arms to help us throughout the journey. While we were at the camp, we also had some training on how to use some of the different varieties of guns and some tactics on how to survive in the wild within enemy lines everywhere. We all got equipped with small arms for the fight if needed.

The detail of the trip and journey was explained to us that there would be at least 14 days, perhaps up to 20 days, and it all depends on what we are going to be facing. Our group leaders stated, "This will not be an easy trip. It will require you to be strong and to stay within the group, pay attention to our lead, you will be facing hunger, and you will be thirsty." He continued saying, "On some parts of this land, you will be facing extreme heat. Unbearable heat during the day, and then extremely cold weather as you climb up the mountain and especially during the night. Furthermore, you'll also be experiencing snow as we get closer to the mountains close to Turkey."

"You need to conserve your food and water and don't waste it. There could be days before you can find any food or water, don't drink or eat unless you are extremely hungry, and when you do, do it a little bit at a time."

He continued saying, "You will have to go through enemy bases as well as crossing the border to another country. And most of your trip will probably be at night to avoid getting caught." He also said we would have to live off the land and eat whatever we could get to save as much food as possible .

He kept reminding us about the weather that we were approaching. "The cold weather, the storms you will go through, desert heat you have to endure while you cross, and even snow, as we approach the high mountains. This is a big land you could easily get lost. If you are not together as a team, you will not make it. It's important you stick together to the end. There will be a time where you will feel like you can't continue the journey. It's not easy and if you are not up to the challenge, don't waste our time and slow us down." I think he instilled so much fear in us that a few of the people with us decided to stay behind. We gathered all of our belongings and made sure there were enough supplies for us to take.

To me, this is my journey. I am ready for the challenge, and I will do whatever it takes to make it.

CHAPTER FOUR

The Beginning of A
14-day Journey

DAY ONE
The Journey

We chose a sunny morning to start our journey. The sun appeared with a cool breeze moving in, and we were ready. But this time, there were over 100 people with us compared to our previous number of 30 to 35 people, so we were ready to start our long journey. We formed one long line with some of our guides in the front of the line and a few more or behind at the end of the line to ensure that we were not separating from each other. I also made sure that the family stuck together, especially with younger children. With over a hundred, our trail was long and organized. I'm very well organized. we took plenty of food and water, and we all had our backpacks filled with all our necessities.

Every time we sat down to rest, we were worried if we were going to have enough food. But we did take a couple of mules to carry supplies for us in addition to what we had in our backpacks, with so many of us, especially families with small children climbing up hills and mountains. Our group leaders separated us with smaller group at the time but not far from each other, especially as we faced rough roads and climbed mountains. The roads were very rough. Our guide continued to remind us that we would take rest breaks as needed but nothing long, and unfortunately, we had to do most of all walking at night so we don't get spotted by the helicopters. They typically monitor the road during the daytime and they don't care if you have small kids with you; they will fire at us. We spent half of the night and day resting by a small river and continued on our journey after midnight. We were exhausted, and after another two hours of walking we decided to rest at the edge of the valley. It didn't take us long until we all fell into a long sleep. Some of us took one-hour turns throughout the night to guard the valley just in case the enemy was close by, and as the night was getting darker, we made our move toward the long valley. We had to be strong, and we ended up carrying some of the small kids while they were asleep. We took turns doing that. Roads were rough until we got to the river, this river with very strong currents with sharp rocks on both sides of the river with no bridge to cross to the other side. The only bridge was destroyed by the soldiers, and the only way to cross the river was a rope from one end of the river to the other end. The rope was tied to a tree, and we had to hang on to the rope with both hands while crossing the river. That was no fun. Few of us had to cross with kids on our shoulders. We made it to the other side with one minor injury to one of the kids who fell off and got swept away by the river's fast current. Luckily we were able to pull him back from the river with some minor bruises and cuts on his head and arm.

We decided to camp there since it was a nice place to rest and the morning was getting close, a good place to rest and wash up. We were able to wash some of our clothes while we had the chance to be by the river. We got some wood fire and boiled water for tea and had some dry bread, and my bread was as hard as a piece of rock. I actually had to soak it in water to make it softer, or we used to dip it in a hot cup of tea to soften the bread. It was nice to enjoy the cool breeze by the river before we had to move again. Another group of people joined us. I found out that they were also from the army. They decided to join us and desert their post, which was close by. Some of them even brought their guns with them. Our group started to ask them some questions to make sure their story was legitimate. They were okay, according to our group leader, so they tagged along with us through our journey.

"We need to stick to each other and be willing to help. After all, we are Kurdish," the older guy with a heavy voice started telling us we must do whatever it took and our mission was not going to be easy, "In order for us to make it, we got to push each other to the limit. This is your first day and there are more to come."

I wonder what tomorrow's day going to be like while looking at these mountains that never seem to end. Despite all that, I was extremely excited not to live in fear and intimidation. We were finally free in our land, and the future looked bright. Not before long, I fell asleep for a short time and woke up ready to go for my next day.

DAY TWO
The Village

As we gathered our belongings and were given instructions on our next journey, all I could see were piles of mountains and hills stretched for miles and miles. Before we took off, we ate plenty of food and made sure there was plenty more food left for the road. We were told that we were going to go to the next village, and we were advised to keep low and not disturb the villagers or do anything to risk the security of people who lived in the village. We kept that in mind knowing how vulnerable these folks are. They endure so much abuse and harassment from the soldiers as they come into their village looking for us.

After hours of walking up mountains walking through long valleys, as you can imagine, having kids with our group made our journey longer.

As we got close to the next village and arrived in the village at sunset, we were separated into a smaller group and stayed at a few homes. The family we stayed with, with the little that they had, still shared warm meals with us. I made sure that we got plenty of food, and they went above and beyond. After a long day of walking, I felt the need to rest and fuel up for our next move because we were told that we had to leave at dawn to avoid putting the villagers at risk. Typically, the soldiers come to the town, often times, harassing people about our location. Our biggest worries were that the soldiers would bring with them Kurdish traitors to translate for them and they were as brutal as the soldiers, and they could care less about their own people. We were told by our leader that every time they capture these Kurdish trators, they are punished severely. They have also captured a lot of Iraqi soldiers, especially those who fled their posts and refused to fight against the Kurdish people. They were treated with respect, knowing that they left their post because they did not want to fight the Kurdish people. Even though a majority of the soldier were Arab, the Iraqi government made sure that the soldiers were deployed to Northern Iraq. "Kurdistan" majority of them were Arab, and a big percentage of Kurdish soldiers who joined their army were deployed to the war zone with Iran. To the Iraqi regime, this was a win-win situation for the government. Kurdish people will fight the war for the regime and die, and the Arab soldier will be in Northern Iraq fighting against Kurdish people assuming Arab people hate Kurdish people, but in reality, that is not true. The majority of Arab people in Iraq sympathized with the Kurdish people and their rights. They did not have much of a choice either. To the Iraqi regime, this is a holy war. Whether you are fighting Kurdish people in Northern Iraq or fighting the Iranian soldiers, you are fighting for a good cause. There was so much fear, so much intimidation, and that was the tactics the government used against their own people.

Also, a big percentage of a soldiers who deployed to Northern Iraq hated the Kurdish people, and they were very loyal to the regime. These were the soldiers that came into the village to interrogate and torture the villagers, they also brought with them Kurdish traitors to translate, and they were as brutal as the soldiers.

Soldiers were brainwashed to believe that this was the holy war. Their mission was to eliminate Kurdish people from existing.

There is so much that we go through and have been through during the brutal regime of Saddam Hussein.

After we rested for a few hours, we got an early wake-up call, and we were told we had to leave because the soldiers were coming to the village. We got up fast and got ready fast. After we left, we found out that the soldiers were accompanied by some Kurdish traitors. As usual, they started harassing the people in the village, demanding answers to where the Kurdish fighters went and how long they had been gone. We advised the villagers to tell the truth and tell the soldiers that we forced our way in by gunpoint and demanded food and shelter and that they had no choice but to accommodate us. We obviously did not want any harm to come to the people in the village. Because if the Iraqi Soldiers found out that they had sheltered us, the soldiers would kill everyone in the village. As a group, we tried as much as possible to stay away from some of the villages. Typically the group leaders sent one or two people to the village that was close to that soldier camp and brought food to us so we were not putting them in danger. Sometimes we just had to live off the land and whatever type of shelter and food it provided. And, as always, enjoy the natural beauty of this land. We did not want any harm to come to any of the people who had sheltered us as we traveled.

In every opportunity we got, we always took the time to practice and train with our leader on how to use our weapons so we could be prepared to tackle any situation. You don't want to give yourself up. You fight until death better than surrendering to the enemy. They will torture you until you die. I had to be alert and aware of our surroundings, ready to do whatever it took to survive and stay alive. What came to my mind over and over again was the amount of strength and courage it takes to survive and be strong and stay strong during this journey with very little experience and supplies. Most of us were from the city, and even though we didn't have the easiest life, we didn't have to deal with hunger and thirst and didn't have to climb up mountains and be on the run constantly, but we needed to do it regardless of all the obstacles and the rough roads ahead of us. I kept my gun close by, and I felt good knowing how to use it.

DAY THREE
Citadel

As we approached this small beautiful town called Amedi. The citadel was built over 1000 years ago, and many of the houses still have their original stonework. This town has many historical sites.

This town and it's citadel was defying everything and stood tall and strong in the face of many empires. The arched stone gate was once the only entryway into town. A large winding stone staircase goes through the wide gate. Since we couldn't enter the city because of all soldiers and their camps surrounding the town, we could only see from far and had to wait until dark so we could continue our journey. Late on that evening, when we could still see the light from the town, we needed to get some rest and shelter from scattered rain, heavy at that time. As we were getting soaked, one of our group members suffered a minor heart attack. And he was in need of medical attention and rest. I have no idea how he survived a heart attack, but there was someone within our group who was in the medical field and was able to perform CPR. We knew we had to drop him off at the nearest village because it was too risky for him to continue to travel. We had to send a couple of our group members to take him back to the village, and we had to use one of the mules to carry him back. We all waited by the cave, and as the dark was moving toward the valley and the rain was slowing, we gathered some wood and started a little fire and, as usual, got some bread and hot tea. Some of us stayed up talking about old times and the city and how much we missed our family and friends, as well as the food. The rest of the group was in a deep sleep. As the day turned to night, it started to get cold, and the darker it got, the colder it became. We didn't have any blankets. All we used were the clothes on our backs and the nearest oval rock to use as a pillow. I kept close to the fire to stay warm during the extreme cold during the night while the rain was getting stronger at the time. It felt good being close to the fire. I thought about all the good food my mother had made. She was an excellent cook, and she always made sure we had enough food that was fresh and hot. All these thoughts crowded my mind throughout the night. I managed to sleep and rest for a little bit.

As the morning approached, we had to pack up and hit the road again, even though we were still tired and exhausted. But we had no choice. The cold morning breeze made it easy for us to continue our journey with little or no food. We knew this would be a long journey, and there was no doubt in my heart that this was worth it.

At the edge of the huge valley, I asked our guide, "Where are we, and how much longer do we have to walk?" He smiled at me and said, "Be patient, son. We will stop and rest." He knew that this journey wasn't going to be that simple and easy. He did not want to tell us the additional details of the journey because he did not want to see us give up, I know it's going to be a long journey and a dangerous one because you are dealing with brutal enemies on all sides of the borders, in fact, on all four borders from the Turkish side, the Syrian side, and the Iranian side. They all had a huge Kurdish community that the government did not respect, and we were hated on all four borders. We stopped for a brief announcement, and we were given additional information about our journey. We were also given some encouraging news to continue the journey. It felt good to me to continue my journey toward being free and toward good opportunity. We all felt good and after a short brief rest, we were able to sit down and share some food with each other.

At the age of this valley, I stood tall and felt extremely good knowing that I was free and ready despite the long way despite all these mountains; yeah, we have to go; yes, we all seem to be ready to do whatever it takes, we all know that this is a huge commitment but a commitment to better future for all of us.

After we took a nice long rest, we all stood up, and we were ready to mark another day. Our leaders ensured that we were all on the same page and encouraged this to continue, but they also made it crystal clear to us that if we decided not to continue, they would be happy to drop us off at the nearest village so we could be on our own, we all seem to be feeling good about continuing the journey. We all shouted, "We are ready!"

DAY FOUR
The River

Our guide gathered us and told us that we would be going across another narrow river that descends with force and strong currents, and the only way to cross it was to use a long rope to be able to cross the river. One of the experienced guys took the rope, attached it to his body, and swam across the river to tie the rope on the other bank. He was a good swimmer and was able to do it fast. One at a time, we hung on to the rope as tight as possible and went across the slippery and wavy river. Each of us had to be careful because if one let go of the rope the river would take you, and there was a danger of getting injured from the huge rocks. As I looked at the rope and saw our guys crossing, I felt good. All the families with small kids were taken by experienced guys. Everyone managed to make it to the other side, and the rest of the group made it as well. The mules that we brought with us made it as well. We were exhausted from crossing the river and in desperate need of food and shelter. One way we could eat was by fishing, and since we had no fishing equipment, we used garnet by throwing the garnet in the river and catching plenty of fish. There are better ways to fish than this, but when people are hungry and have no choice, they do whatever it takes to survive. We ate plenty of fish and got plenty of rest, but it wasn't long before we heard the sound of helicopters flying toward us. We knew immediately that we had to hide fast. The two helicopters came close to us, and they started to shoot at us. We scattered and ran for cover from all directions. I could hear the kids screaming at the sound of the helicopter and the big gun they used. It was one scary moment. I ran as far as I could and took shelter behind a rock. Some of us started to shoot at the helicopters with our pistols and AK 47. That wasn't a good idea because that made it worse for us, and as a result of shots being fired, a few of our guys were wounded. After the helicopter left, we gathered to evaluate the damage and treat the wounded guys with whatever medical supplies we had. They needed help, and we had to get them to the nearest village fast. We also found out that two of our guys went missing in action. We conducted a thorough search to find them, but there was no luck. One of the guys said, "The two guys who are missing are the ones who informed the soldiers about our place." We all looked at him and asked how he knew that. He replied by saying, "I heard them talking on the radio, but I was not sure, and I didn't want to get involved." At that point, the guys who were in charge of us started to interrogate him and took him to the side where we couldn't see much. They brought him back, and he admitted that all along, he knew about this. He was part of it. They handcuffed his hand with a rope and tied him down, and he was beaten and would be dealt with once we arrived at the next village. He was handed to Kurdish fighters, who took him to the base and locked him up. Traitors like this guy put all of us at risk. We almost lost a couple of our guys. Too bad the other two guys slipped out before we could find them.

We sat on the bank of river and jumped in for quick wash and washed all my clothes. We were able to get some rest, food, and water at the village, and our guide gathered us and informed us that there was yet another long way ahead of us. He also mentioned that those of us who wanted to stay behind should do it now. There will be no looking back. We all stood out there, knowing we did not really have a choice. We have to do this. A big storm was heading our way, with the wind blowing very hard, and the pine trees were making a loud noise. "It's going to be a big storm," the old man shouted. "Get ready to move so we can get to the end of the valley, where we should be able to hide in some of the caves from the storm." We moved slowly toward the huge valley, and our trail was a long one. As I looked back, there were almost 100 of us. Some people joined us, and some left us. I kept asking myself *I wonder how many more days we had to walk*. But that's what kept me going, the idea and hope of knowing that I would finally be free one day, where the future looked bright. I had been through a lot of suffering in my life, and knowing that I would one day be free kept me going.

DAY FIVE
The Storm

The rain started to come down very hard and it made everything slippery. Having a family with a little one with us, we needed to find shelter, and our only shelter was to get to this huge cave that was at the edge of the mountain. This was not easy, especially having some of the families that needed help with the kids, the ground was getting muddier and harder to walk on. We covered our supplies from the rain and by the time we got close to the cave we were soaking wet, and with the evening approaching and the darkness moving in we had to hurry fast and make it, or else we won't. The storm was getting stronger, and the rain was just pouring in nonstop, which made the ground muddier and we saw a huge pile of mud coming down from the top and quickly getting close to us. We had to make it to the cave; otherwise, we would get buried in mud. This was not an easy task, and the cave seemed to get further from us, or at least it seemed that way. "We gotta move fast. We're almost there," shouted one of our guy. By the time we got to the cave, we had noticed some of our guys were missing or left behind. I was one of the guys who went back to look for them. They were stuck in the mud and hiding behind a huge tree holding on to the branches. We managed to pull them and walk up slowly, and one by one, we made it to the cave. Luckily, there was plenty of wood that we gathered, and we built a big fire to dry our clothes and make tea and enjoy our lovely hard dry bread. Some of our guys stayed up talking. I was so tired and laid down to sleep,but the thoughts of my family kept me awake. I was thinking about my family and what they have to go through. My mother, in particular, was on my mind knowing that she was worried about me. She cared about us and worked very hard to raise all 9 siblings. My mother worked throughout the day she was something like a nurse by trade, not school. People trusted her to take care of them. She would travel to people's homes to take care of the sick and prepare their medication which was an all-natural remedy. There was something magical about her touch, her approach, and the way she healed people, all-natural. She has helped so many sick people. I remember this guy who got burned, and the hospital gave up on him and sent him home after they tried everything with no luck. They called my mother to go to their house and take care of him. My mother was there every morning for hours, taking care of him using natural herbs and applying them to his body. I was with her helping her mix natural herbs and mixing them. I was twelve years old when I noticed, after weeks of treatment, this guy was getting better and was able to function on his own. That was my mother, she was well-trusted by people, and she helped anyone that needed help, and people paid her money for taking care of their loved ones.

My mom worked and made money to support us and even bought land for us to build a house. She had money saved up to send my older brother to college to pay all his expenses. On the other hand, my dad wasn't much help and wasn't aware of my mother's extra funds. He knew she worked and made money, but not about the extra. My father was a small-time merchant that sold anything and everything. He sold tobacco in the black market which he smuggled from different towns, and I remember when he used to take my brother and me with him to help smuggle tobacco. What he did was he used to hide it in the clothes we wear along with our coats hat had deep pockets, and he would stuff the pockets with tobacco. When we get to the checkpoint coming back, the officer typically doesn't check in the kids. We got away with it, and then my dad sold it on the streets, and he was always on the watch for the police. He got caught many times, and each time, he must bribe the officer so they can let him go. He didn't make much money, and we didn't see much of him. He was always out of town, either bringing products to sell or visiting friends and family. People thought he was an angel, he was well liked by people, and people thought he was really funny, but at home, he was a different person, and nobody knew that side of him. At home, he was very abusive with a super short temper and oftentimes, he took his anger out on us, especially my mom, and as we got older, we always protected our mother. My memories of him were all about consistent physical abuse. There were times when he was nice and understanding, especially if he had the money and the market was good for his products that he sold.

I still loved my dad despite what he put us through, "May God forgive him."

We were very scared of him he was very abused physically and emotionally, and as we got older, we started to defend our mother everytime he was beating on her and it got so bad were we wished and prayed that he would die and never come back again. Every time he was out of town, we enjoyed being home without him. My mother took excellent care of us. When my dad was home, it was a different story unless he was in a good mood, but we feared him. He always carried an AK 47 bottom folded so he can carry it under his coat. He had many enemies because he was involved in killing due to revenge. He was also involved in politics and was in jail a few times, and even got tortured by the government. He always wants to be ready. I remember my older brother came home from school one day all beaten up by the teacher because of not turning in his homework on time. In those days, teachers were allowed to use a stick to hit students. Until it was banned around 1970. My dad went to school with his AK-47, and I happened to be with him. He pulled the trigger and aimed the gun at the teacher. The teacher got on his hand and knees crying and begging for his life ,my Dad told the teacher, "If you ever touch my son again, I'll put 30 bullets in your head. Did I make myself clear?" The teacher promised my dad never again. I remember the teacher was so scared, he wet his pants. That was my father, very brutal and aggressive. "May God have mercy on his soul." My mother put up with him and I remember when he died, she didn't shed a tear at his funeral.

I kept thinking about my mom, and I knew her faith was strong, and I knew the rest of my brothers at home will take good care of her. My mother was at least 15 years younger than my father. We are a big family with 2 sisters and 7 brothers. One of my brothers was in living in the USA after the collapse of the Kurdish revolution in Northern Iraq. He was accepted as a refugee in the USA and moved there in 1974. I knew the government always harassed us about where my brother was and if we had any contact with him, and now with me out as well, I know they will be harassed by the local government. With all these thoughts, I fell asleep for a few hours before our next move.

DAY SIX
The Deep Open Valley Walk

We were informed that our next move would be a full day through the roughest and driest land. "There will be no water or trees but desert mountains," the old man shouted. This is a long stretch with what seems to be the never-ending valley. Despite the rain we had yesterday, it seems that the valley sucked in all the rain. We got plenty of water to carry, hoping that would be enough throughout the day especially knowing that we were going through this valley that was surrounded by mountains, so everything was trapped within the long valley.

We were advised not to finish the water fast and to drink it only when resting a bit at a time, but as we started to move, I noticed some of our guys were going through their water fast, and at midday, when the sun was burning hot, and we started to slow down and rest. Every time we stopped, we were going through water fast and at one point, I shared my water with one of the family and that felt good sharing, but that was until we ran out of the water I felt that I should have saved my water for a later time. We were exhausted from the heat and lack of not having enough water. Some of us had to stay behind and rest more, especially the ones with the kids. Our guide kept telling us to continue moving. There are some broken wells at the end of the valley, and if we move fast enough, we might get there before the night moves in. What a dry piece of land. There is nothing in this valley besides snakes and lizards. I almost got stung by a rattlesnake, but I was able to kill it. By the time we got to the end of the valley, we were ready to give up hope. We were thirsty and hungry, and all I could see was the long valley surrounded by dry mountains which trapped all the sun heat with no trees to hide under. What do we do when we are in desperate need of water and food? We must continue to get where the water is, and according to our guide, the water is close by, and to give up faith. We finally found the water well, but it was deep, and we couldn't reach it, so we used whatever container we had to scope the water at this point. No one was concern about the quality of the water or the sanitation level. In fact, one of our guys was so desperate he used his shoes to scope the water out and drink it. There was plenty of water for all, and we rested by the well for a few hours. We had a good rest, and now we had to look for some food. There wasn't really much to look for beside some bread we all put together and shared among all of us. The good news was that we had water and that was important. We rallied as a group to discuss the rest of the journey, and that meant another few hours of walking to the next village, where there would be food and shelter. We were so hungry that we shot at a few birds and were able to kill some birds and immediately build a fire and enjoy bird kebab. We made sure the younger kids had some to eat. When hunger and thirst hit and you are trapped in the middle of nowhere, you will do anything to survive. It's brutal. I was able to get a bite, but our priority was to feed the kids and diabetic comrades. Now we have some strength to continue the journey, but there is always that hope of getting to the next village. I think that's what kept us going. By the time we got close to the village, we had found out that a group of soldiers was harassing the villagers about the rebel base, and they were also looking for us, we stayed outside side the village, not knowing how much longer, but we had to stay calm. We didn't want to put the people at risk. These are some nice focuses, and if the soldiers find out that they sheltered us and provided food, they will be tortured and harassed. We were able to move in slowly toward the village, one group at a time. By the time we all got in, it was dark, and we were ready to get some rest. Some of us took turn guarding and securing the entrance to the village to make sure no soldiers were coming in. We took turns every hour and shared a secret password in case anyone tried to get in. We were ordered to shoot if needed. This was one way to ensure our safety. It was one scary hour for me because I was all alone, and I could hear the sound of crickets and the darkness. I had to make sure I was awake to ensure our safety. For soldiers to come out during the night is rare and if they do, they always bring with them some of the Kurdish traitors who sold their honor and dignity for the money. We were able to get some rest. The sky was clear and full of stars, and there was no trace of the moon which made everything so dark.

A cool breeze was moving, which made us comfortable to relax. We set off early in the morning, and our exhausted feet led us through the long journey.

DAY SEVEN
Crossing The Border

Some of the families stayed behind because some of the kids were sick and needed rest. We started our journey not knowing what was next on the agenda, but we kept moving. Every time we stopped to rest, I tried to eat as little as possible and save some for a later time. There wasn't much food besides bread and some dried beef, similar to beef jerky; because of the heat, the bread was moldy, and I typically take the mold off and spray some water on it so it can get a little soft. Again we were advised to save some of the food for a later time, and that is what we all did. "Save water and bread and keep thinking about the long journey," the old man continued saying, "Save your water." The next two days will be a long, and we have to cross the border to Turkey, the only way to continue our journey. The reason we have to go through Turkey and circle around the mountain was that there were many Iraqi bases around this area, and to continue without interfering with the soldiers, we had to take the risk of going through Turkey crossing to their border back and forth to make sure we are not getting spotted by either of them.

We are ready to fight if we get confronted by the enemy. Through a narrow dirt road, we started going up the mountain that I couldn't see the top of. This was a very rough road that had these narrow trails that only rebels used to cross the border. I like to make it clear to the world that we are freedom fighters, simple people who want to be free after what our people have to go through for years and years and still going through it. So much fear and so much pain that Kurdish people have to go through.

Our trail was long, with all of us in straight line, with one after the other. I found along stick to use as a cane to help me climb up the mountain. We were advised that every time we hear a helicopter or jet fighter, to hide and avoid wearing any red color or any other bright color and to also put our any fire wc build because we can get spotted easily with smoke from the fire. We actually saw a few helicopters flying near. Of course, they were looking for any sign of attacking us, but we kept low. As we approached the top of the mountain, the wind was fierce. It was a bloomy cold day as the light of the sun was disappearing and reflecting from some of the snow-kept mountains, making it very cold. The old man said, "There is always snow all year long from the winter. It gets so cold there that there are patches of snow. It gets extremely cold, especially during the night, all over the mountain, and as the winter season approaches, these mountains get covered with snow throughout the whole year. You can still see the snow on the top of the mountains during the day. It gets a little warm, but never as much as it was when we were in the valley.

Crossing the border to Turkey, a different country, is not an easy task. You are not only breaking the law, but you are also dealing with another government that hates Kurdish people and their huge Kurdish population that live in Turkey, so we had to be careful crossing the border and avoid Turkish Soldiers. At one point, we were so close to the Turkish border patrol that we had to hide and stay low until they passed us. We stayed on our border and waited; one of the guys was telling us they were looking for Kurdish fighters from the region of Kurdistan in Turkey. So there we are, dealing with 2 different regime that hates Kurdish or anything that has to do with Kurdish. The goal of our mission is to get to Iran. There is also a huge Kurdish population in Iran, but Iran had some sympathy for us because we were fighting the government of Iraq, and since Iran is currently in a war against Iraq, that made us welcome in Iran.

The road was long and dangerous, and the mountains were full of sharp rocks, which made it hard to go up the mountain, especially during the night. All we could think of was water and food. We had no strength or energy to move. We all crashed at the edge of the mountain, exhausted, not knowing how much longer. One of our guys was shouting hard, so I got up from deep sleep, and it was morning already. I must slept for a few hours. We got absolutely freezing weather and bare minimum clothes we had to cover ourselves with. Thank God for the fire we built throughout the night that kept us a bit warm. I woke up from a deep sleep. I believe it was for a few hours when we heard one of the guys shouting, "It is time to get up. If you need to make your hot tea, drink it fast."

Moving fast during the day was the key to making it faster to get to a safe zone.

Our guys spotted a shepherd at the bottom valley with a lot of sheep. I'm done. I mean, we could purchase a sheep or two since people were in desperate need of money. We gathered some money and approached the shepherd, and offered the money for either a goat or lamb or both. The shepherd was happy, and we picked 2. We then immediately started a big fire. I didn't butcher the goat, but I watched a few of the guys doing it. We were so hungry and starving that it was the best meal we had ever had, an especially hot meal with a lot of protein that'll keep us going for miles. We even managed to take some with us for the road. The good news was, there was a stream of water running through the mountain, so we were able to supply up and wash up. It was really hard getting on the road after all the food that we ate, but we knew we had to keep going with the long journey ahead of us, especially not knowing what was next. At this point, all we knew was that we would be hitting one of the biggest mountains. It almost took a full day to get there. This particular mountain was at the edge of Turkey, Iran, and Iraq. We started to walk slowly, and the wind picked up. As we went up, we went from warm weather to extreme cold and colder as we were getting higher you can even see that most of the mountains were full of snow.

Our group got spotted by some Turkish soldiers, and they started to shoot at us before we even crossed the border. Our leader made us break into smaller groups, and we retreated back to our base to regroup again and waited for the right opportunity to cross again. We waited almost all night, dealing with severe cold weather. We were able to build a fire in an orchard which was located near a running water wheel. We sat and cuddled under a huge walnut tree and around the fire, which helped us stay nice and warm. The sky was clear and full of stars, and here we were at the top of these quiet mountains overlooking two borders of two countries that hated Kurdish people and everything that had to do with Kurdish. At the corner sat an old man with a lot of really good stories, always ready to be shared. He started telling us about this brave Kurdish fighter by the name "Mahmood Yazadi," who was a great fighter who fought and died for our land. The old man raised his head toward us, he was showing signs of sorrow and sadness. We saw that through his sad smile. Talking about a comrade that left a huge mark throughout this land. He continued telling us about this wonderful fighter and all of the missions he carried out, and most of the time, he was alone to fighting without fear or anything. "Let me tell you about some of his mission," taking a deep drag of the hand-rolled cigarette, "He undertook military mission and seized many weapons. The government pushed hard to capture him with no luck. They put a price on his head, dead or alive." The old man took a deep breath and reached his cold cup of tea, and added more hot water to it, "Yes, he was a brave fighter that had no fear, and he was determined to do whatever to bring the enemies to their hand and knees, on many occasions, he disguised himself as an army officer and walked into the enemy base and killed many of their officers and seized some of their weapons and destroyed some of the heavy ones."

"The government feared his name, and soldiers were afraid of him. He carried out many successful mission, and the government was willing to do anything to capture him, and their only solution was to get Kurdish people that knew him and by offering rewards, the few Kurdish who sold themselves and worked with the government. These traitorous mercenaries sold their soul and dignity to the enemy."

The old man took a deep breath and said, "Yes, he was killed after an informant that was working for the government informed them that he was in a neighboring village. They sent the whole army to arrest him. He killed many of them and was able to make it out of the village alive when he was cowardly shot by a Kurdish traitor. We were shocked and disappointed," he said, "but we got that son of a bitch and made sure he paid the price."

"I'm so glad they captured and killed that traitor."

As the fire started to die down, we added more wood to it and fell asleep with the thought of that great fighter.

DAY EIGHT
The Long Border

At an early hour of the morning, as the sun disappeared in heavy clouds, we set off to hit the road. This time, one small group at a time, and we were given instructions to stick with our group until we got to our destination, "There will be a long stretch on the Turkish border because you got the Iraqi camps all over this side of the border," he took a deep breath and said, "so stick together and help each other out." It was especially hard as we were able to see the Iraqi soldiers and their camps. It's a nerve-racking situation where you know once you get seen by the soldiers, then they will start shooting at us. We also don't have much choice on the other side of the border because the Turkish soldiers will be firing at us, and either way, we are in a tight spot. As we broke into smaller groups and we walked slowly and eliminated all bright colors so they will not noice us. After hours of walking, we were advised not to cross the border because of Turkish soldiers at the border town. We waited a few more hours. Unfortunately, that was the only path that we had to take to make our journey. On our border, there were the Iraqi camps monitoring the mountains by helicopter and the Turkish soldiers in the north of the border monitoring their border. We didn't have any other way to do this. This was the only way to make the journey. We had to deal with so much throughout the whole journey we had to make sure that we were taking good care of the sick and some of the families with younger kids. We also had to worry about some of the guys within our group, especially not knowing they could be working with the Iraqi regime. Our group leader made it clear to all of us that if we got caught as a traitor, we would be killed. I had a good feeling about our group this time and especially after we caught the last guy. I felt especially good knowing we were getting close to our destination and as I looked back, crossing the border to Turkey, I saw a beautiful land with beautiful agriculture that has so much to offer anything you can imagine is available. We have deserts, mountains, rivers, and very rich agricultural land. This land is surrounded by regimes that hate Kurdish people, and the thought of Kurdish people having their own land one day made these government regimes very nervous. The thought of having Kurdish lands and a Kurdish country that is run by Kurdish people, these regimes could not tolerate, and they were going to do anything and everything to destroy our land.

At last, we were able to cross the border to a small Kurdish village from Turkey. The leader of the village was under tremendous pressure not to Harper any Kurdish fighters, but he was nice enough to supply us with some supplies. We managed to rest for a few hours under severe cold and frost weather that was even worse at night, we were so exhausted and weak that we rested and were able to stay close to keep warm, and we even built a little fire to beat the cold. I started thinking about what the future will be holding for me and where I will end up after this journey. I knew I had to stay strong and healthy. My dream of a better future and better life kept me going despite the pain and suffering. Our future and our youth were all spent in fear, and as a teenager in Iraq, you don't get to enjoy all of what other teenagers throughout the world experience. My teen and my time since I was 12 has been very rough moving from location to location and always hiding and pretending that you love the government and love the leader, and there's always that fear of intimidation, but we still made the best out of it and enjoyed being around friends and family.

Some of the best times Kurdish people had in Iraq was in March 1970 when the Iraqi government announced a peace plan providing autonomy for Kurdish people. The plan was to be implemented in four years. In the first year or two, we felt more free. We were able to move freely without any fear and intimidation. Kurdish people felt that they had rights and as the nation was coming together, Kurdish and Arab people started to feel that it was possible to live peacefully together. It felt so good as Kurdish during the peace treaty. It felt good, and everything was going in the right direction. Prosperity and jobs were available. We even had our own Kurdish newspaper in our language, as well as a television channel. Unfortunately, in the 1970s, the peace agreement between the Kurdish and the Iraqi government did not last long, and the Iraqi government in 1974 began a new offensive against the Kurdish people. Our Kurdish government was engaged in a war against the Iraqi government. I remember we got assistance from Iran since they were enemies with the Iran government during the Shah of Iran government which they were a great ally to the United States of America. We got support from the world, and our fighters did well controlling the northern part of Iraq, but after that Iranian government signed an agreement with the Iraqi government, the Iranian government stopped helping and supporting the Kurdish people. We were no match for the powerful Iraqi military and we were outnumbered. All Kurdish people were pushed to the border of Iran, where we stayed in Iran as refugees. My family ended up as refugees in Iran, and after spending 8 months in Iran, we came back to Iraq after the Iraqi government assured all the Kurdish refugees were allowed to come back to Iraq, no questions asked, and assured we would not be harmed, thousand and thousand of Kurdish people came back to be refugees in their homeland. My older brother stayed in Iran. He didn't go back with us. He was a high-ranking officer within the Kurdish military and feared that the government would kill him. When we went back, all the Kurdish were placed in different towns and cities, we were under watch constantly, and we lost everything we had. We lost our home, and now we live in a shack, ten of us living in a home built out of mud. The village we lived in was 45 minutes away from the city of Mosul, so my older brother and I decided to go to the city to continue our education. My older brother was accepted to go to the university in the fall for engineering, and I was still in junior high school. We rented a small room and both us worked in construction during the day; and I managed to go to school in the evening. We helped our parents and siblings by sending money back as much as we could.

The year after my brother moved to a different city to attend university, I stayed at my uncle's. They were very generous and supported me. I still had to work odd jobs to help my focus.

I moved from one relative to another, and they were all accommodating to me. After two years, the rest of my family moved back to the city, where we all lived together again.

Monitoring any uprising movement and we were under constant watch .

To me, there was always that hope of coming to America. That was what kept me going and pretty much motivated. I watched all American movies and Western movies, including Western spaghetti movies. Some of my favorite movies were movies like West Side Story, Rebel Without A Cause, and of course, Saturday Night Fever. As a teenager, you see these movies, and you compare your life to theirs and hope you can live like that and have a good quality life and be free. With all these thoughts occupying my mind, one of our guys shouted, "Stay strong and keep going even though on an empty stomach and weak body." "Rest, my friend", the guy shouted, "we are getting closer and you are becoming stronger and better. Keep going." It wasn't easy passing through two brutal enemies, the Turkish and the Iraqi, and here we were, facing the danger zone and going across the border on some of the rockiest and the coldest mountains. Hope for a better future was what kept us going.

DAY NINE
The Storm

"Get as much rest as you can," the old man shouted loudly. "Our next point is on the top of one the highest and coldest mountains in Kurdistan". We all started to get worried, especially knowing there may be a storm up in the mountain. As we are getting close to the fall season, it gets extremely cold, especially being so high up. Lucky for us, we managed to get some heavy clothes to keep us nice and warm during the night.

One of the comrades stood up and pointed at the top of the mountain, took a deep breath, and said, "Let me tell you about our leader, our father, our brave leader who conquered these mountains and fought against the brutal regime. With only a hand full of men, he set off through Kurdistan, and his movement began to gain strength and became stronger and widespread." "Our leader was well known to the world and refuse to give up, 'Mustafa Barzani' was a Kurdish leader, our leader who was one of the most prominent figures in the world. A leader who led our revolution and stood against the Iraqi regimes all the way to the end."

We continued listening to him talking about our courageous leader that fought hard, and his dream was to one day be able to have our own land, our own country, "Kurdistan."

Kurdish people have suffered so much throughout the years and still suffering. "Why couldn't we live peacefully like any other nation? Why couldn't we be free and be able to travel freely anywhere and everywhere without fear?"

After some rest, we got together for instruction on how to deal with the storm if it got in our way. We can still see some of the snow on the top of the mountain despite the thick layer of clouds. We started to move slowly toward the top, and it was getting colder as we were getting closer to the top. Visibility was getting harder and it was hard to see, and as we were expecting, the cold wind was starting to pick up and the storm was moving in as we got to the top. Our leader advised us to hold hands and not to lose each other. We all made it to a cave that was buried with freezing snow, where we were able to get some water from a little spring inside the cave. At this point, we were so cold even inside the cave, and our leader asked us to start moving down, otherwise, we would all freeze up here. We lined up and started moving down with the strong wind, and after a few hours of exhausting up and down the mountain, we made it to the bottom where there wasn't as much snow or wind. As we were taking a tally, we noticed two of our guys were missing, and it was most likely that both guys got stuck in the snow, especially with almost zero visibility, someone needed to go back and check, and we decided that the two most experienced guy should be heading back looking for them. The two guys left, taking one of the mules with them. We knew it would be a while before we could hear anything. At the same time, we all were praying to God and hoping they can be found alive. It was a long day of waiting and not knowing, and then all of a sudden, from a distance, we saw the mule. As they were getting closer, no one was prepared to see two bodies on the mule, both frozen to death. It was a sad day after getting to know both guys so young, and one of them had kids left behind. We cover both bodies and our leader wants us to give them a burial on the next village, which is close by. We got to the village late and we spoke to the leader of the village, informing him that we had two dead bodies and we needed to bury them as soon as possible. Arrangements were made, and they were buried on the same day. This part I wasn't used to seeing or used to, it's not easy burying your friends, especially in the middle of nowhere with their family members not aware of their death. I'm sure someone will have to inform their families. This is the price of freedom. I would die here with dignity rather than getting caught and tortured by the worst regime in the world. I have my gun in my hand, and that means I will fight to the last breath before I can surrender to the enemy.

DAY TEN
The Deep Valley

I see this enchanting nature and this beautiful land deserted. Its inhabitants have left a long story, a long struggle with many sad stories to tell. Everything here has been destroyed.

It was hard to continue our journey knowing we had lost two friends, but we had to continue on our mission and according to our leader, there were only a few more days left in our journey. A long valley was ahead of us, we can still see some of the snow on the mountain top, but it was not as cold as being on the top of the mountain. I still had the toothache that I experienced days back, but it wasn't as bad before as it is today. Today, the pain is getting worse and unbearable with no painkillers or dentist around. The only option was to wait until we got to the next town, which is a few days away. My toothache was getting worse by the minute. I felt I should just have it pulled. At the next rest, one of the old comrades approached me and said, "I have an idea that will help ease the pain." At this point, I'm willing to do whatever it takes. He then built a fire and put a needle on the fire for a good 10 minutes until it got red and asked where the tooth was, and after I showed him, he asked me to open my mouth and had a couple of the guys hold me down. He then placed the tip of the needle on my tooth. I actually felt the chiseling and the sizzling as he placed the needle on the painful area. He repeated the process a few times. At this point, I don't know which pain was worst, the toothache or the burning, but I felt a huge deal of relief especially after part of the tooth broke. He continued to stick the needle for a few more times on the root or the gum and that soothe the pain.

The group was exhausted from the long journey, and by the time we got to the end of the valley, it was dark and the cold wind was moving in gradually. Our leader recommended that we stay at the valley to get some rest, so we can continue another long journey in the morning. I felt much better, especially after we found out that one of our friends had some painkiller. I believe I took 3 Aspirins and that helped with pain, even though the pain wasn't not as bad. I also couldn't eat anything besides some soft bread, which I had to soak in water so I didn't have to chew, and that wasn't easy.

DAY ELEVEN
The Cold Murder

As we gathered in the morning to make our move toward some of the roughest roads, where one can see a long narrow valley surrounded by a tiny sharp river that cuts through the valley. "Only a few more days comrades, and we should reach our destination," shouted the old man. That sure made us very happy to hear that. We stopped at the request of one of our guys. His wife was pregnant and was not feeling well, so they wanted to go to the nearest town, which was further down from our destination. One of our guys volunteered to escort them to the town. We started our journey slowly cutting through the valley, resting whenever we could and snacking from some dry molded bread that we carried with us and got used to. On occasions, we enjoyed some of the food nature was offering, from certain grass and plants that were edible, and of course, the tea that kept us going. The wind was picking up and the cold breeze was moving in gradually as we got closer toward the mountaintop. It was a beautiful scene. Looking at the river cutting through the valley with the sun laying at the edge of the valley. You can see the layers of the sun disappearing as the clouds starting to cover it. "This will be the place to camp for the day," said our leader. We gathered our belongings and started looking for food; some of the guys gathered some wood fire, and others started looking for food from the plants and some other type of grass. We shared what we had and made the best out of it. As usual, we all sat around the fire to keep nice and warm. It was late in the afternoon, when a man from the village was passing by, asking if we knew the husband and wife that separated from us. We said yes and told him that they separated from us to go to the town because the pregnant lady wasn't feeling well. The man said they were found murdered. That was shocking and very sad, knowing they were such a loving couple and they were looking forward to their baby. How could someone do that, and why? We immediately knew they were murdered by the guy who volunteered to escort them. A few of us went back to care of their bodies and escorted it to the nearest town with a proper burial. They informed the villager at the town about the murder, and gave a description of the coward who murdered these innocent folks. He had also raped the lady. Her clothes were all torn and bloody." He will not get away with this," our group leader said, loud and clear. "He will be found, and he will pay for what he did," It was a sad day for all of us. We lost the whole family. We lost a good friend. How could someone do that? And why? We paid our respects, and all of us prayed for the family.

DAY TWELVE
"Another Innocent Comrade In My Arms"

After, we suffered a harsh night from the cold and rough night, grieving our friend and his wife, who were murdered by the coward who fled the town.

On this beautiful morning, the sun was warm and shining in the warm embrace of nature. As we continued our journey to the nearest town, this town was a Kurdish town belonging to Iran, so we were in a different country, and the pressure of not dealing with the Iraqi regime was a breath of fresh air. The first thing I did was, to find a dentist to take care of my tooth. The pain was still there. The dentist pulled the tooth out, and that's exactly what I needed to ease the pain and continue on my journey. We gathered for a meeting with our group leader, to let us know what was left of our journey. He mentioned that the town we will be going to, is on the border of Iraq and Iran and the name of the town is "Ziwa", and that was where most of the Kurdish refugees live, as well as the leader of Kurdish people. He also mentioned that some of the Kurdish people from Iran that live in the town had struck a deal with the Iraqi government to dig the body of the legendary leader, Mustafa Al Barzani, who was buried in the town for big prize, so we were asked to protect the body and guard the graveyard as well as find those Kurdish terrorists who are responsible for an act like this. We all decided to volunteer for the mission and stormed the little town that those terrorists lived in. Then after a long battle, we managed to drive them out of town and kill several of them, and in that process, we lost one of our friends he was shot in the chest. We carried him to the mosque, and I watched him die in my arms. The last thing he gave me was a picture of his two boys, and he told me to tell his kids that he loved them and was very proud. It was tough and hard losing a good friend. After the burial, we managed to send a message to his spouse with some money to inform her that her husband died with honor and dignity.

It's been a long journey, and we have come a long way. Sometimes people don't know how good they have it until they've been through what we have been through, and that sure makes you appreciate what you have. Today, I feel stronger and happier, and appreciate what I have and what I have accomplished. I am proud of all the lessons of life and all that I have been through. Despite the suffering, I feel great about all my accomplishments.

DAY THIRTEEN
"Hardships Of The Road"

We gathered with our group to discuss the final preparation for the final town, and that was a full day of walking. We were exhausted from the long journey and everything we had been through. This was one long journey that I will never ever forget. This truly shaped me and made me appreciate how precious life is. This is it. The town is on the other side of the valley — I'm free, my friend, no more fear.

With all the difficulty, we set off through this deep valley. There is still snow accumulated on the edge of the valley. Despite the weak morning sun, the weather was cold, and I was shivering from the cold. We continue walking while trying to keep our bodies warm in order for us to reach our destination. I kept thinking about a good meal and a good night's sleep. I'm not sure what that looks like anymore, sleeping in fear for a few hours during the day and a few hours at night, especially not knowing if we are going to get attacked by government soldiers,we always have to be ready to run before getting captured. Being at the border and close to Iran, we felt a little safe, and since we didn't join the fight and fought against Iran during the war between Iraq and Iran that lasted 8 years, that made it easy for us to settle in Iran as refugees. There's also a huge Kurdish population that lives in Iran, which has been mistreated by the Iranian regime and is going through what the Kurdish people in Iraq is going through. Today we don't like to cause any problems in Iran. We're going to stay as a refugee and do our best to get out of the country for a better life and future.

We camped at the edge of a valley a few hours away from the town, and after hours of walking, we reached a point of exhaustion.

Evening comes, and the sun begins to disappear, and sunset disappears behind the mountains, leaving a pretty bright spot at the edge of the valley like it's been dyed by an artist. This is a good spot to spend the evening and cattle around a big fire that we built to keep us warm during the cold night.

DAY FOURTEEN
"The Arrival"

On a slightly warm morning, the sun came out weak after a harsh cold night. We needed some relief from the cold, and since there weren't any heavy clothes beside the clothes on our backs. Much of what kept us warm was the fire we built throughout the night that allowed us to cuttle around the many fires we built, and we stayed warm.

As we approached the town, our final destination was finally a good night's sleep and decent food. The town that we were getting to stay in was a big town with some shops and tea shops where a lot of refugees spend most of their time sitting in the shop all day drinking tea and talking politics. It was a wet day as we approached the town. We were also greeted by a group of people that showed us where we would be staying in the camp. The camp was decent, with two sections, one for families and one for singles. During the time we stayed in the town, there wasn't much to do besides just sleeping, eating, and passing the time. I also kept thinking about the friends we lost along the way and especially that coward who killed the innocent family. I hope he will get caught and be executed. I know that we will not rest until he is found, and there will be no place for him to escape. The Kurdish Authority and the Iranian Authority were given a full description of the suspect who killed the husband and the wife after raping her. We were informed after a week that he was found at the bus station around the city of Tehran, the capital of Iran and was captured. I know he will get what he deserves, and I thank God for that.

For me, the plan was to get out of the country, since we arrived from Iraq, and now we are in Iran, and we are considered refugees here, and as long as you respect their laws and don't cause any trouble, you will be treated well, that was my intention. Iran was going through major changes throughout the country, with very tight security everywhere, especially with the new Islamic regime led by Ayatollah Khomeini. They were cracking on any movements against their regime and against those people who were close to the old regime the Shah of Iran, Mohammad Reza.

The situation was extremely difficult, and to get out of the city one needed a special permit and money, which I didn't have, and connection that I didn't have either. Most of the Kurdish refugees stayed at the town with plenty of food and shelter and much of activities. I was determined to find a way to get exposure outside the town and work toward continuing my journey. As a refugee, it made it even harder to get permission. It took me some time to get permission so I could travel to a nearby city and apply at the United Nations office for asylum outside Iran. I put our names down and went back to the town. We were told it would be a long time before we could get the answer. Meanwhile, to stay busy and keep moving, the Kurdish authorities in that small town were all the refugees from Iraq. Pretty much all the Kurdish refugees, the Kurdish official who was in charge signed all of us to join the training camp. There's a training camp to get us ready and train on how to use different weapons. The goal was to get us ready in case we had to head back to the mountain and get back into fighting using weapons and tactics to become freedom fighters. A lot of our guys signed up to stay back and go back to Iraq and defend Kurdistan, our region. I continued training every morning and throughout the day, and we were back at the camp in the evening to take shelter, eat and sleep. I stayed out of town for almost 2 months, then one day, my cousin who lived in the nearby city came to visit me. I was very happy to see him. He invited me to go and stay with him in the city that he lived in. He applied for a permit for me to leave the refugee town. What was nice about our training at the refugee camp it was not mandatory. We joined the training, and it was a good program in which I personally learned a lot. I was able to got a permission also from the official at the camp to leave with my cousin, and after we got permission to leave, my cousin and I took the bus to a big city called Esfahan, a nice and beautiful city. From 1592 to 1722, Esfahan was the capital of Persia. I truly enjoyed staying in the city. It was absolutely beautiful, covered with beautiful hand-made tiling and the magnificent public square. This magnificent public mosque in the city dates back to 1628. It is regarded as one of the masterpieces of Persian architecture of Iran.

I stayed with my cousin, his wife, and their baby, they took excellent care of me, and I was treated well.

My cousin knew that my plan was to go to Europe, and he was willing to help me. My cousin Mageed was an excellent merchant, buying and selling and doing everything he could to make ends meet. After staying with him for quite some time, I was able to get my passport from Iraq. My brother sent it to me with a trusted friend who was able to deliver it to my cousin. My passport was valid, and that meant I am able to travel to nearby countries like Syria, Turkey and anywhere in the Middle East without a visa or a permit as long there is a valid passport.

I was also told it would be easier to go to the capital of Iran. Tahran and fill out an application from the United Nations office for refugees. This will be my second attempt to fill out an application. I filled out one at a small town near the refugee camp, but being in a big city like Tehran may make it a little easier to hear from them faster. People were saying that it's much easier to apply from the capital and the process is faster.

My determination and commitment to Europe and America. After what I had been through during the 14-day journey, I've seen so much. I need to make it to Europe and America, no matter what it costs.

Money was tight, but my lovely cousin took the initiative to accompany me to the capital city of Iran.

PART TWO

'JOURNEY TOWARD AMERICA'

Being in Iran in those days was very difficult, especially with the new regime in power and the security personnel who were all over the city cracking on anyone and anybody who seem suspicious. It was just like living in Iraq all over again different regime but the same mentality. The street or patrolled very tightly and you have to have documentation with you at all times. You could not do anything that much, especially when you do not speak the language, but what really helped us was that we were Kurdish from Iraq and carried arms and fought against the Iraqi regime, which made it a little easier for us. Just like they say, "The enemy of my enemy is my friend." I had my documentation with the permission to travel with my dear cousin Majeed, who was a refugee in Iran and spoke the "Persian language," which is very similar to Kurdish language and I can easily understand some of it. My cousin went out of his way to accommodate me. I stayed with him and his family at that time. They had one child. He kept me with him on days when he had to work. I stayed with his wife. My cousin was very hard working in order to support his family and he always made the time to take me around the city he lived in. I will forever be thankful for everything he did. It was able to extend my permit to stay with him while he helped me get more exposure to the city and all the foreign offices to submit my application for a refugee status in Europe and America.

We traveled to Tehran, the capital city of Iran, where I could go to the United Nations and apply for a refugee status. I had no money to take the bus to the capital city, but my cousin Majeed took time off of work and accompanied me to the capital city. Traveling from one city to another city in Iran is the exact same as in Iraq we went through many checkpoints, and at every checkpoint, we lined up with our paperwork and my case permission. There was zero tolerance for anyone who did not have the right documentation. I experienced seeing people who were taken outside because they looked suspicious to them. When it was my turn, they examined my permit over and over again, and started asking me questions, and they did not want my cousin to interfere with their conversation with me. My cousin told them that I didn't speak the language and that he needed to translate, and after a long conversation with the officer, they finally gave me my paperwork back and stamped the paperwork. We went through more checkpoints with many of the Islamic Republican guards all over each checkpoint who were ready to crack against any movement against the Islamic regime. They were looking for people who were associated with the old regime in the shaw of Iran since the majority of those who were loyal to the shah of Iran already fled the country. They only took as much money as they could with them. The government were confiscating all of their wealth, and those who stayed behind lost everything, and some will even put in prison. The guards were also looking for any sign of womenswear to make sure they were completely covered by Islamic rule. The guard even had a brush and paint. They had a few women lined up who forgot to get part of their legs, it was not covered properly. The guards were using black paint and painting their legs with black paint. All these women were begging and crying for mercy. A short time ago and during the time of the Shah of Iran, females in Iran lived and enjoyed the freedom of the Western World. They had the freedom to dress up any way they wanted and wished. Some even wear the veil and covered their hair. After all, it was their choice, and it was not forced upon them. My mom always had her hair covered, not because she had to but because she wanted to.

Seeing all these tragic scenes, there was chaos everywhere. And by the time we got to the capital city of Iran, Tehran, we saw a beautiful modern city with a lot of high-rise buildings, and nice streets, but there was so much fear and so much intimidation that you always felt that you are walking on eggshells. My cousin and I stopped for a late lunch after a long ride we spent the night at a hotel. Even the hotel was guarded by the security guard. To me, this was exactly how we lived in Iraq, a similar brutal government that did not care about their people. Being a Kurdish citizen made it even harder to live in both countries. A huge Kurdish community in Iran as well, are under the same pressure and abuse just like the Kurdish people in Turkey. The Kurdish in Iraq and Syria, were always considered second citizens.

The following morning, we got up early visiting the United Nations office. The line was long, it was hundreds of people who have applied. I approached the clerk and gave him all the information about seeking asylum in Europe, hoping from there I could make my way to America. It was forbidden to mention the name "America". People in the street were shouting "Death to America!" and this was during the hostage crisis where they saw the embassy and detained 50 Americans. Iranian militia hated Americans, but I believe the people of Iran did not have a choice, but to march on the streets and burning American flags.

On my application, I did not dare put America as one of my destinations. The goal was to get to Europe and from there, I will definitely make my way to America.

The application process was too long and the representative from United Nations told me that it was going to take a minimum of a year or longer to get my application processed. This means that I have to stay here and get a job in a tight market. I'm not able to speak the language.

On the way back, we took the bus again heading to Esfahan where my cousin lived.

After we came back, I was able to tour the city by myself while my cousin was at work. I met a Kurdish guy from Kurdistan of Iraq, and his name was Semko. He was in a similar situation like me, and wanted to travel to Germany. He was looking for a partner to go with him. Semko has never been out of the country before, and he only spoke the Kurdish language. He told me he needed to find someone that can help him translate as they travel. I told him I spoke Arabic, fluent Kurdish and spoke a little English as well. My new friend has money, and enough of it to travel out of the country. After I explained my situation to him, about not having enough money, he agreed that I go with him and use his money because there was no way he could travel on his own; not being able to speak the Arabic language and English. You can travel all over Middle East speaking Arabic but Kurdish language is just spoken in a few countries. I was able to get some money from my cousin Majeed. Despite how tight a situation was, he insisted on helping me.

After doing some research and how to get out of the country, we found out that we could travel to Syria, which was a great ally of Iran and Iraq. We also did not need a visa to travel to Syria as long there is a valid passport. So my friend and I purchased two airline tickets to travel to Damascus, Syria. The tickets were not very expensive and the flight was short. On the day of our departure, I thanked my cousin and his family for the great hospitality. He was there for me and I'll forever be thankful to him and his family.

We took a cab to the airport and as we approached the security personnel to have our passports examined, they sent us to a special room, a secondary area, and started interrogating us. They couldn't find anything wrong. We were both refugees and we had our valid passport. After being in the interrogation room for some time, they finally stamped our passports, and we were able to catch our flight. This was my friend's first ever flight, and we were happy to get out of Iran. We are going to Syria, and from there, we will work our way going to Europe. As for me, my final destination will be the United States of America.

Damascus, Syria

We landed in Damascus, the capital of Syria. The regime in Syria was very similar to the regime in Iraq. They were both brutal governments. They also had a nice grip on their people and their freedom. They had tight security everywhere and it seemed like everybody was watching you, especially since we came from Iran. All four countries, Iraq, Iran, Turkey, and Syria, hated the Kurdish people. Constantly living in fear on all four borders was one of the reasons why we wanted to get out of the country. So we can seek a better life, so here we are in Syria, and since I spoke the language, it was easier for me to navigate through the city with my friend. Semko was holding on to me since he did not speak the language, so I assured him we would be together. We managed to keep low and stay low. After all, we were here for one reason and that is to get out of the country as soon as possible. We were very happy to land in a city that will be our ticket to Europe. We didn't have much money to travel, and we needed to figure out ways to earn more money, so we went to the flea market, where we met a guy who was crooked and was trying to convince people how to double their money by playing a simple game. He knew that we were not from Syria, noticing my friend's accent while he was talking to me. He invited us to join and play the game. We fell for his dirty trick. We stood out there watching people play, and they were winning big time, so I convinced my friend and told him, "Let's play. It's easy to win," not knowing some of his customers that were participating in his game were in the same gang. Their game was a trick, an old gambling trick. They do it by gathering people, and unbeknownst to their prey, the majority of the players are part of the trick. They worked together to trick people in the game called *Belt Game*. They used a belt or strap folded in half and wounded it with a coil, inserted a stick into the center loop, so it remains inside the belt when unrolled. The operator tricked us and told us that we had lost. An old trick which we fell for, and we ended up losing some of our money. Luckily, we pulled back and decided to leave after the police came and busted some of the guys, but for us, it was too late since we'd already lost some of our money. I felt so devastated, and it was all my fault. Here we were on our first day with very little money and had already lost a big chunk of it. "Lesson well learned." Good thing we still had some money left with us, maybe for another week or two.

The plan from now on, is to save as much cash as possible. We were eating as little as possible and stayed away from restaurants. As the night approached, we looked for the cheapest hotel that we could stay in and finally found a beat-up motel with a reasonable rate. Right now, the only concern we had was where to get a job, any job, so we could save money. Both of us have the energy and the drive to work hard and do whatever it takes. At least we feel a little safer here.

Our game plan was to make it to Germany, and in order to make it there, we needed to purchase an airline ticket that would take us to East Germany. In East Germany, you did not need a visa. All you needed was a valid passport so you could travel to East Germany. You can stay in East Germany for 24 hours only, and from there, we can travel to West Germany.

East and West Germany and the city of Berlin were divided into East and West Berlin.

First, we had to get to East Germany, where we were only allowed to stay for 24 hours. After 24 hours, we had to either go back to where we came from or go to West Germany, according to a lot of friends and family members who made it to West Germany, the same route we were planning to take, once we land in East Germany. When we arrive at East Berlin, we take the train heading for West Germany. When we get to West Berlin, we surrender to the authorities as refugees. In West Germany, they would never force you to return, especially if they knew that you have a good case and you are from a country that does not respect human rights.

That was the game plan. Money is tight. We had enough for a week or two, but we needed more, so we needed to look for a job as soon as possible so we would be able to purchase airline tickets. Money was our biggest obstacle and we didn't have enough to pay for the tickets. We had to spend our $200 wisely since it was the only money we had. We even bought food from the market and started to cook it at the motel just to save money. As the days went by, it was very hard to get a job, especially not knowing anyone and not having connections. I approached the owner of the motel one morning and asked him to help us get a job. After revealing our current situation to him, he agreed to give us a job at the motel. Cleaning rooms and maintaining the pool, in exchange for a free stay, was not much of an offer, but that was better than nothing. We worked like no other workers for long hours on certain days, and the owner noticed how dedicated we were, so he decided to give us some extra cash, and his wife brought us food daily. A very nice lady who told me, "You and your friend that doesn't speak any Arabic are wonderful people and you are making our job easy." The owners of the motel were in their late 60s. They were doing most of the work before we started helping them with everything. From cleaning to repairs, they were very happy with our job and we felt pretty good being there, earning some money and staying at the motel for free. We were able to save whatever money we had left, but still, it was not enough to buy airline tickets, so we looked for another job besides the one we had. One day at the motel, we met this guy that was in a similar situation. He was from Kenya, Africa. He had the same plan to travel to Germany just like us. He told us that he was going to another city in Syria called *Latakia*, found in the Northwestern part of Syria on the Mediterranean. According to some of his friends, it was much easier to get a job there and make more money. Jobs there were hard, and most of the jobs were either working in the fields, picking up lemons and oranges, or working at the shipyard, loading and unloading goods bound for shipment. After meeting this guy, we were convinced that we needed to do the same exact thing. Move to the city of Latakia and find a job. Breaking the news to the owners of the motel was going to be very hard because they got used to us working hard in maintaining their motel.

We decided to leave and take advantage of the situation. After all, we were barely surviving and unable to save money.

We informed the owner of the motel and he wasn't too happy about it. He even offered us more money to stay in the motel because he liked how hard we worked for him at such low compensation. We thanked him and his lovely wife for giving us the opportunity to work and stay in the motel. After telling them that we were leaving the motel, they assured us that we could come back anytime and they would help us with anything we needed.

THE CITY OF LATAKIA

The following day, we said our goodbyes, packed our belongings and left the motel, and headed for the bus station, where we purchased our tickets to Latakia City. The fair wasn't as expensive, and we still have some money left. The journey from Damascus to Latakia was about a few hours. It was a beautiful ride, and we witnessed beautiful sceneries throughout the trip. There were mountain ranges and a field of orange citrus. The city was well-known for producing tobacco. As we enjoyed the scenery from Damascus to Syria, there were a few checkpoints, but they were not as strict as it was in Iran or Iraq.

We arrived at the city of Latakia after a long ride. Beautiful city on the Mediterranean with a wide open sea that was new to us since we had no sea in Iraq. Enjoying the great weather and the beautiful scenery, we spent a few hours touring the city and even dined in a nice restaurant for the first time, where we had a hamburger and fries and that was the best ever. As the night was approaching, we were looking to secure a cheap hotel or motel, and after we looked all over the place, we found a decent hotel. The owner only accepted a weekly rate, and we were fortunate enough to have enough for a month, which we gladly paid. The hotel was decent and small, and they even had a community kitchen where you could cook. Our plan was to start hitting the ground running and looking for a job. We spent the following day getting to know the town and looking for a job. We gathered at this cafeteria where typically foreigners will gather looking for a job. It was like a local job market. They come in looking for workers throughout the day, but your best option is in the morning and early morning.

People sit there all day drinking coffee and tea, and the owner depended on foreigners to earn money. As long as you buy something to eat and drink, you can stay all day. We got up every morning around 5am and went to the coffee shop, waiting to get a job. Typically, odd jobs could be a few days or a few hours, or if you are lucky, you get a contractor with a big project that may last up to two to three weeks. At this point, we were willing to take anything and everything. Chances of getting picked for a job was good, but you have to show willingness and commitment, and that you are ready. We were ready.

Our luck came in for us one early morning, when a farmer came in with a big truck and shouted that he was looking for a few workers to work in his citrus fields with oranges and lemons. We were so desperate and eager to work and get a job, so we were the first ones to be at the front of the line for the job. While the guy was still talking about the details of the job, we were already ready for work. The owner noticed how dedicated we were and how ready we were, so he immediately asked us to get on the truck while he was getting a few more people. We did not even negotiate how much he was going to pay us. Getting in the back of that truck with my friends, I felt great that we have the job. There was at least 12 people in the back of that small truck, holding on to the rail of the truck and we were on our way to the field.

THE FIELD OF ORANGES

The job was on the outside of the city, where the field sat on a huge land surrounded by miles of orange trees. We got dropped off and were given instructions on what the job was all about. The old man was very clear and straight to the point, "You will be picking up oranges and dropping them off in a big container. You will be on your own, but I expect you all to fill up all the containers at the end of every day's shift, which is 10 hours in a day."

"Are there any questions?" he asked and then continued saying, "Yes, you will be having a one-hour break. You can bring your lunch daily, or I can drop you off at the nearest restaurant." Since we didn't bring any lunch today, we asked him to drop us off to get lunch. He also told us, "You can eat as many oranges as you can, but don't get sick on me." The job was hard, but it was a piece of cake for us, since we have been through so much. We were actually having fun. I have never in my life eaten as many oranges as I did on the first day. The owner stopped by once every 2 hours, laughing and telling us to go easy on eating oranges or else we were going to get a stomachache. The owner was also stopping by to provide us with water, and he also gave us a large hat to wear to protect us from the sun. The owner brought us lunch as a treat on our first day, and it was a generous portion of rice, soup, and lots of bread. It was extremely nice of him to do that. We worked harder to show him that we truly appreciated what he did.

At the end of our 10-hour work, the owner dropped us off at the cafe and told us he was extremely impressed with our work and that he would like us to keep working for him. We were happy to know that we have a job. All we have to do is show up in the morning at the cafe to get picked up. Our payment was given daily. The job at the orange field was going really well. We worked six days and enjoyed one day off, which we mostly spent at the cafe, meeting locals and making friends. On several occasions, we got invited to homes where we enjoyed a nice home-cooked meal. Time went by, and we were saving as much money as we could to purchase an airline ticket, but we still had a long way to go, so we just kept looking for another job.

One late afternoon, we stopped by a coffee shop to get coffee and sandwiches, and we met this guy, who was looking for people to work in the shipyard. He was handpicking people who seemed to be strong and they were mostly from Africa. We approached him kindly and asked if we could be given the opportunity to be part of his crew. He checked us out and he flat-out told us, "You guys are too skinny and weak. There isn't enough muscle on you to handle the job." He looked at us and pointed to a group of African men and mostly from Nigeria. "Chad and Somalia are over 6 feet tall and look strong. These are the kind of men I need on my team to unload the ship, and I'm sorry you are not going to cut it. You guys are too weak." The guy absolutely made us feel miserable and useless, but we are going to continue our effort in looking for a better job that pays more money.

I looked at my friend, and I think he understood what the guy meant. I told him not to worry. We are not giving up so easily. These guys may be tall and strong, but they didn't have the commitment and the drive that we had to make it through all the situations that we've been through. We can do this, especially knowing that the pay was twice the amount of money we were making working in the field. As the foreman was making his selection, he was only picking the tall and strong, and I felt like a weak dog who would be left behind because I was not barking hard enough and not showing signs of strength. After all, this was like an arena where only the good and the strong survive. I approached the foreman and told him, "Don't let our look deceive you. We are strong and I'd like you to give us a chance. You don't have to pay us on the first day if you think we are not suited for the job. Give us a chance. Let us show you who we are. I guarantee you, you will be impressed and we will get the job done, so what do you have to lose?" I guess we got his attention since he went ahead and asked us, "So you really want to work under the condition of not getting paid if I'm not satisfied with your performance?" "Yes, we are willing to do whatever it takes to prove to you that we have what it takes, and if we don't meet your standards then, you don't have to pay us. All we need from you is to show us how the job is done and a little patience because once we do the job, you will be impressed with our level of commitment, hard work and enthusiasm."

He gave us a funny look and reached out, touched my shoulder and arm, looked at me and said, "I'm going to do this for you guys, but keep in mind, this is a big ship and requires hours of work. I will try you guys for half the day, and if you don't meet my standards, you will have to quit and go that day." "No worries, we will do it, and you will be impressed." Then he went on to explain the scope of the job and how much money we will be making. He continued saying how the job pays and in my mind, I was shocked. "This is what we make in three days on the orange field; we can make it in one day." The problem with this job was that it was only three days a week, and it depended on when the shipment arrived. We asked our boss if it was okay with him if we worked only three days in the field, and he was okay with it. He even told us to come to work whenever we felt like it. The following morning, we got up around 5 am to go to work. So we met at the coffee shop to get picked up for work. There were 15 guys, including us. A huge shipment of bananas was waiting for us. It arrived from South America with thousands and thousands of boxes of bananas that needed to be dropped down to be picked up by trucks. I have never been so excited about work, especially knowing the amount of money we were getting. We worked so hard for almost 10 hours, and we were able to take breaks and rests. At the end of the day, the foreman was delighted with our job and assured us that we would be on his list for the next shipment. By the time we got home, we were soaking wet and absolutely exhausted and when we arrived at our hotel, we cooked and ate. After long hours of hard labor, we had no problem trying to get some sleep. In fact, after we ate, we immediately hit the sack and slept like a baby. We got up early the following day and went down to the cafe, and had a heavy breakfast. We also took some lunch with us for our lunch break. We got picked up by the foreman and headed straight for the shipyard. First, we gathered for a little meeting with the foreman. The manager who was in charge of our group had nothing nice to say besides yell and scream about zero tolerance for laziness on the job. He assured all of us that he would have no problem letting us go if we slacked. During the first few hours of work, he was constantly yelling and screaming at all of us using profanities, telling us in the Arabic language that we were a bunch of slaves. He was having a bad day and I don't know why. He was rude and unappreciative; deep down inside, I did not pay attention. All my friends and I did was just work non-stop. We took breaks as needed, bathroom breaks as needed, and our lunch. The manager kept checking on all of us, and after he saw how hard everybody was working, he calmed down.

During our break and time off, we got close to the rest of the guys on our team. Some of them spoke Arabic, and some spoke a little English. They were all from Africa. They were some of the most hardworking people I have ever met. They flee their country, seeking a better life. The majority of the money they make, they sent it back home to their family. In the meanwhile, we managed to keep both jobs, the only problem working in the shipyard was that it was only two to three times a week, but having both jobs, we managed to save money.

One day, I spoke to my friend and told him that I needed to speak to the foreman. The manager of the shipyard was becoming very abusive toward all of us. No respect for any of the workers and everybody hated him, but we did not have a choice, but work because the money was good. The manager was never happy, regardless of how hard we worked. He didn't care about our work. He kind of knew that we did not have a choice but put up with his aggressive behavior. He was just ready to boil over for some of us. He did not appreciate how hard we worked, the constant profanity used, insulting us, and calling us a bunch of lazy slaves. At this point, I think I had it, and I wanted to personally approach him, since I spoke the language pretty well. My friend Semko joined me. I approached the manager at the end of my shift in a place where I asked if I can meet with him one on one. He was actually pretty nice and agreed to it, and even got us a cup of tea each. I think he knew that we were not pleased with him, and since none of the other guys ever stood up against his unacceptable behavior. We were extremely nice and polite as we started the conversation. We told him that we do not appreciate the constant yelling and screaming at us, the constant abuse, and the infinite use of profanities throughout our shift. We told him that if he was not happy with our job, he could just tell us to leave and we will be more than happy to do so. We work very hard and put in more than 100%, and we want you to treat us with respect, not only us but the whole team. I felt really good taking that out of my chest and standing up for what I believe in. After all, money is not everything. The manager looked at us, surprised. I don't think anybody has ever approached him and spoken to him the way we did. He told us that he has a great deal of respect for all of us, and especially us, because we work really hard, but he has a lot of responsibility in getting the job done in time because there is a lot of pressure on him as well. I told him we can still get the job done but approach the people in a nice way so we could feel good about ourselves. I also told him that we'd been through a lot. My friend and I came from Iraq. We were Kurdish, we were a freedom fighter, and we have been through a lot of pain. The minute we mentioned we were Kurdish, he immediately told us that he has so much respect for Kurdish people. They were the hardest working people in the whole world, and personally, he loves working with Kurdish people. After all, there is a huge population of Kurdish people in Syria.

After we had our last long conversation, his attitude completely changed, and he started to be nice to all of us. He was still being hard and pushy, but he was totally okay. At least he was nice about it. Our crew worked even harder to produce better results, and the manager noticed that he didn't have to be so mean and intimidating to get results.

The work situation was getting better every day, and we started enjoying the job more and more. Despite how hard and difficult the job was, working 10 hours in the shipyard, at least the level of respect that we saw from the manager got better, and in return, we did our best in doing our responsibility and made sure that we were working even harder to avoid disappointing our manager.

As time went by, we managed to have one day off between both jobs. We worked more at the citrus field and worked at the shipyard sometime up to three days a week, and all depended on when the ships arrived. On our days off, we went to the beach, we took the city, and we met plenty of friends there. We could not get enough of being by the beach and the beautiful Mediterranean Sea. There were also a lot of tourists from all over Europe and other Middle East countries. Where we lived in Iraq, there was no sea and only the rivers, so being on the Mediterranean Sea was a treat, and the weather was absolutely gorgeous.

After almost 2 ½ months of hard work, we managed to save enough money to purchase the airline ticket but at least that's what I thought we had enough money to purchase the airline ticket. We got permission from both jobs to travel to Damascus. Both jobs assured us our job would be there when we came back; we wanted to make sure just in case we decided to come back that our job would be there and there might be a possibility in case the money was not enough.

We went back to Damascus, the capital city, to purchase our airline ticket. Little that we know that the airline tickets were extremely expensive, especially if not purchasing tickets in advance. We had enough for the ticket but needed more for pocket money in case of an emergency. Purchasing an airline ticket in advance could have been a lot cheaper, but we did not have the money to purchase the tickets now. We were almost paying double. I told my friend I was going to have to call my brother in the United States of America, who's been living there since, so I called my brother and my lifetime friend. He was exactly like a brother to me. We grew up together, and lived together, and everyone we knew, knew us as brothers. I spoke to them on the phone and asked them if they could wire us some money as soon as possible. It is nice to have a family member that is willing to help you at a moment's notice. $500 was sent to us Western Union, and that was a lot of money at that time, enough to purchase the airline ticket enough to have pocket money. I will forever be thankful for their generosity and open heart despite their tight situation in America. They were both going to college and working as well as supporting their family, and they still managed to send the money to us.

After we purchased the airline ticket on the following day, we stayed at the motel that we worked at when we first came to Damascus, and the owner was extremely happy to see us and he was happy that, we made enough money to go to Europe, he did not even charge us for the night to stay at his motel.

The following day we took a bus to the airport, but before we did that we called both jobs and Latakia and informed them we were not going back. We arrived at the international airport in Damascus, ready to take off any minute, and we were so excited we did not even have any luggage. We each had a small backpack with a few clothes, and we did not get all that we wanted to get out of the country and go to our destination.

I believe this was one of the happiest moment in my life getting out and going to a country that respected human rights. A country were you have the right to speak your mind, where you are treated fairly. I have heard many, many stories from friends and family members about how good is to live in Germany, Sweden, and the United States. Pretty much all the Western countries. As we got to the airport, the line was extremely long for both ticket prices and the security checkpoint. We made it through the security checkpoint since we had no luggage. We all had one small bag, which made it a little easier for us, when the time came for them to check our passport, the police officers took both of our passports and went through each and every page, especially the passport being from Iraq, but before that, we were advised that the police officer are very corrupt. We were told to put money in each passport, no questions asked, so the process much easier to stamp our passport and board the airplane, we managed to put a $50 bill in each passport, and it was a lot of money at that time; once the officer opened our passport on the side of the $50 bill, there was a huge smile on his face and he immediately stamped our passports, and he was very nice and wished us good luck.

Government officials are corrupt and are willing to do anything for money. As we boarded the plane we were both excited and nervous, excited about our new future and nervous about what's ahead. For us, it was time to celebrate as we got on the airplane. This was one happy moment for us. We had unlimited beverages on the airplane. We enjoyed a nice meal. The flight attendant is very happy to hear our story. She made us feel very happy during the flight. I believe it was a few hours, and as we got close to landing in East Germany, we were excited about what was next.

EAST GERMANY

We landed in Berlin, East Germany, not knowing where to go, and the people at the airport were not very friendly. All we wanted was to cross to West Berlin. We only had 24 hours to either go back to Syria or to West Germany, and of course, going back was not an option. People in this particular city seemed to be extremely quiet like they wanted to be left alone. We are surrounded by extremely tight security with German soldiers all over the streets carrying their guns, watching every move and ready to shoot anyone that crosses the wall to West Germany, it looked extremely simple extremely easy, but nobody can dare to even get close to the wall, I heard several stories of people got shot and killed. The Berlin border crossing was created as a result of the post World War II division of Germany. At that time, West and East German were treated very differently when entering or leaving east Germany. West Germans were able to cross the border relatively free to visit relatives. East Germans were subject to far more restrictions.

Finally and after wandering in the airport for some time, we were able to find our way to take the train (Autoban) that traveled to West Berlin, and communist East German soldiers heavily guarded it to make sure none of their citizens would cross. Their soldiers well known to shoot any of their citizens crossing, but for us, they can care less. As we landed in West Berlin it was a different story. People were alive and active, and the city was the most beautiful I have ever seen, with joy and happiness, and finally, we are here in the land where we are free. After all of the abuse we experienced with our government in Iraq.

We strolled in the streets for hours. We managed to grab a bite to eat and went to West Berlin, where it was so crowded. People seemed to be very happy. Boys and girls were holding hands. Kissing in the street. Things that we've never seen in Middle East. You are not allowed to hold hands and kiss in the street.

We were overjoyed to be here. We were able to go to the nearest police station to ask for asylum and give ourselves up, and to our surprise, they would not take us, but instead, they gave us the information about the place we needed to go. We took a cab to the immigration building, where we were given temporary identification and shelter to stay in. One of their gated buildings accommodated refugees, a big building where hundreds of people stayed until the case was done. We were given a room with three other people, so four people occupied one room with bunk beds and three meals daily. We were advised that we were not allowed to leave the camp to go to town, unless we got permission or got invited by someone from outside. The camp was a little bit far from town, and we didn't have any money, so we stayed at the refugee camp, where there were plenty of activities that we could do from playing football, playing cards or watching TV.

On weekends, we were allowed to experience and visit the city, but one needed to get permission. On weekends, they were a little easier on us. I knew we were able to ask permission to go to the city.

We managed to stay within the facility of the asylum, where we felt comfortable and everything we needed was provided to us. I knew a few Kurdish people that lived in the city of West Berlin and actually, few of my cousins who have been in Germany for quite some time now. One of them was a professor at the university who was able to come in and get us out of the camp. He introduced us to a Kurdish community, where we were able to get some exposure to different offices to process our paperworks a little faster. We were also able to get a permit to leave the camp and visit the city. We spent majority of our time in one of the Kurdish refugee offices who were advocates for Kurdish refugees. After a few months, we heard from that refugee agency, and we were able to attend a meeting, and they invited a translator to translate from Kurdish to German, and they approved our case. It usually takes years for some people to get approved for asylum, not unless you have a solid case. In our situation, it was a lot easier for us. After all, everyone knew that these people have been abused by their government, and they were mistreated by the government, and to top it off, they were sending us to war. It was easier for us to go outside, which I was glad that we finally got and that means that we can finally be free to move around and get a job. Since there were so many refugees in West Berlin, we were not allowed to stay in West Berlin. The officials were dividing all the refugees, and they were moving them into different cities, different towns in West Germany, so they can control the flow of refugees. We were sent to a small town close to Stuttgart, where we were guaranteed housing assistance from the government and help in getting a job. We did not have much of a choice. We had to leave, especially since we were getting assistance from the government of Germany. After all, we are happy that we are in Germany. I personally did not want to leave West Berlin, because I have a lot of friends and family members that lived there and were willing to help me.

Finally, the day for our departure to our new home came. We arrived by the small town with a very small population. Majority of the people who lived in this town were German, and there was hardly any foreigners besides a few Turkish people, who has been living in Germany since the end of World War II. They had a lot of businesses. After an hour, we arrived at our new place with three of us living in an apartment with one bedroom and one bath. To us, this was absolutely perfect. It was more than what I could ask for. We appreciate everything the government gave us and all the assistance at all times. They took to get us exposure to work at job sites, and we were given the privilege to go to school and learn the German language and everything else we needed to know about the country. It was crucial for us to learn how to speak German since hardly anybody spoke English, so you had to learn the language. Our life was pretty good. We lived pretty comfortably. We were able to cook on our own. We permission from the government to go out and explore our small city or town. It was the cleanest city I have ever seen in my life. It was so clean and organized. On weekends, people would volunteer to clean the streets. Everything was picture perfect. Majority of the people in town were quite, and also did not like foreigners. We were being discriminated. We could not go to the bars at night, and there was always a weekend demonstrations against foreigners to express to us that they want us to leave their country. Oftentimes, it was me and my friend on the streets, buying or doing other things and we hear a lot of people telling us in German "Ausländer raus" meaning "foreigners out." Sometimes during the night, we could not go out and be alone without group of friends together with us. We were afraid that will get beat up and harassed. Berlin was totally different, it was a bigger city with more foreigners and refugees. We felt much safer there. In this small town, the population is small, but a lot of original German folks lived here, however, not everyone in this town was prejudiced. Majority of the people are extremely nice, and have accommodated us. In fact, they was a German professor who visited us weekly, and invited us to his place to help us learn the German language. A lot of nice people went out of their way to accommodate us. I know it's not a big percentage of German who lived in town that hated us.

Little by little, we started to learn German. We even met some friends that helped us. I was lucky enough to meet this young lady by the name of Claudia, we became very good friends. She would often visit us, and she even spoke a little English, and as time went by, we got closer and became best friends. She took me and my friend out dining and exploring the town. We had so much fun being friends, until one day, her father knocked on our door and brought translator with him. Even though I spoke a little German, he insisted on bringing someone to make sure I get the message. As he walked into our apartment, the translator to explained to me in English, that I needed to leave his daughter Claudia alone, and not to ever see her again. He told me that she was only

17, and that she does not need a refugee like me to be her boyfriend. He was furious, and was shouting in anger and I pretty much understood everything he had said even without the translator having to translate for me. "You must leave Claudia alone, and you are not allowed to talk to her ever."

I told the translator to tell him that we were just friends. She was just a sweet young lady, who has been helping us tremendously, and we were getting along really well, and that I would hate to lose our friendship.

After the translator explained to the father what I had just said, the father replied and said that if I don't leave his daughter Claudia alone, he will report me to the authorities that I was harassing his daughter. Then they would take my refugee status away from me, and they will ship me back to Iran. He made it crystal clear. At this point, I told the translator to tell him that I would be more than happy to leave his daughter alone, and I could assure him that nothing ever happened between his daughter and myself. We were just very good friends. I was afraid, and now I don't want to lose my refugee status and deal with this angry prejudiced man that did not like foreigners. I surely did not want to go back to Iraq and go through what I had been through again. Going back to Iraq it will mean death, especially after deserting the army. The father left, but before he did, he said, "Last warning. Leave my daughter alone."

Claudia tried to contact me a few times. We've gotten a little closer to each other during the past month or so. I met her one time after the conversation with her dad and told her what had happened and how her dad threatened to send me back to Iraq, and as much as I hate losing our friendship, I asked her to leave me alone. I didn't want to get in trouble with her father, I totally understood, and since she was only 17, it made it really hard for her. We ended our relationship, and we kept in touch with each other over the telephone, every once in a while.

It makes me very sad we are all human beings, and we all have feelings, and when we end up meeting some people who are so prejudiced and disliked us for who we are, it makes it very hard for us.

My game plan was to go back and live in West Berlin, so I contacted my cousin and a few of my friends, and they were willing to accommodate me and help me get a job if I decided to move back to West Berlin and that I will be on my own. At the time we lived there, we got assistant for everything, but I was determined to move back to a bigger city, where I can pursue my goal of coming to the United States. My dear friend Semko was able to get a job and a restaurant as a dishwasher which she was extremely happy with. I informed him that I would be going back to West Berlin to live there and asked if he wanted to go with me since we'd been together for quite a while now. He insisted on staying in the small town. He told me he had just got a job, and he was happy. There was also a Kurdish community in that town where Semko, my friend, felt comfortable. The same Kurdish community that helped him with everything that he needed to survive in that little town.

I told him that I would miss him and I would definitely come back and visit, and if he ever decided to move to West Berlin, he could come and stay with me at any time. After all, we had been through so much, he and I.

I packed up all my belongings and took the bus, said goodbye to my friend, and assured him that I would keep in touch for a long time. In fact, we have kept in touch throughout all this time. I arrived in Berlin, and my cousin was waiting for me at the bus station, I stayed at his place, and with my permit, I was able to look for a job, and with the help of my cousin and some friends, I landed a job working for the city as a street sweeper from 6:00 in the morning until 2:00 in the afternoon, the pay was pretty good and enough to survive. Typically, jobs like that are ones that German people will not work it, so they leave it all to the foreigners, who are ready to do any kind of job after all we appreciate we have a job.

I met a friend of mine whom I've known from Iraq. We grew up together, and he has been living in Berlin for more than 3 years. His name is Safar, he was fluent with the German language and had a good job, so I moved in with him and his girlfriend. They have been together for almost 2 years. My friend Safar helped me a lot, and he was able to help me get a better job with much better pay since he knows a lot of people.

I was in constant contact with my brother, and I was trying to help me to immigrate to America by sponsoring me, I was able to be granted an interview to immigrate to the United States of America. I was asked to go to Frankfurt at the American consulate. They even paid for my airline ticket, I went to the airport after I got my ticket, I got the airport late, so I stayed in the hotel in Frankfort which was close to the American consulate. The day after that, I went for my interview, I was also provided with a translator who was Kurdish from Turkey. While I was doing the interview, I was having a hard time understanding the Kurdish guy who was translating from English to Kurdish, I understood the

American guy more, than the guy who was translating to me from English to Kurdish. The Kurdish language in Turkey was sometimes harder to understand, they use a different dialogue than the Kurdish language from Iraq. I was having a hard time understanding this particular guy. I requested from the consulate if I can just speak English, instead of Kurdish, and without the translator, it would be much easier for me. He agreed but also kept the translator just in case. I was able to understand every question he asked me, and I was able to describe the reason why I was seeking asylum in the United States. He was extremely impressed with my knowledge, knowing so much about America and the history as well. The interview went really well, and he assured sure that I would be hearing from them. Special thanks to the Lutheran Church. The church is the one that sponsored me and paid for my airline ticket, of course with the help of my brother as well.

I returned to Berlin, and after 2 weeks, I heard from the American consulate. They have approved my application, and they mailed me my new identification.

That is the best news that has ever happened to me. Finally, my dream came true. After living in Germany for 18 months, I left on March 7, 1983 and landed in New York City on March 7, 1983.

I took a deep breath as I got off the plane, and as my feet touched down at the airport, I felt freedom. I felt my dream had finally come true all my youth. I have always dreamed of coming to America and knew in my heart that I would like it to happen someday. Here I am today, feeling tall and strong with a sense of accomplishment. Today I celebrate March 7 as the mark of a new beginning and new opportunity that I was given. Today as I look back at my long journey and what I went through, faith and hope kept me going, and I know in my heart that I will make it. Today I look back at my hard journey, I am happy to say, "You can accomplish anything you want, if you put your heart into it."

CPSIA information can be obtained
at www.ICGtesting.com
Printed in the USA
LVHW072337200723
752881LV00014B/174